Golf FOR DUMMIES®
POCKET EDITION

by Gary McCord

Look for Pocket Editions on these other topics:

Allergies For Dummies, Pocket Edition
Anxiety & Depression For Dummies, Pocket Edition
Asthma For Dummies, Pocket Edition
Dieting For Dummies, Pocket Edition
Heart Disease For Dummies, Pocket Edition
High Blood Pressure For Dummies, Pocket Edition
Menopause For Dummies, Pocket Edition
Migraines For Dummies, Pocket Edition

WILEY

John Wiley & Sons, Inc.

Golf For Dummies®, Pocket Edition

Published by
John Wiley & Sons, Inc.
111 River St.
Hoboken, NJ 07030-5774
www.wiley.com

For general information on our other products and services, please contact our Customer Care Department within the U.S. at 877-762-2974, outside the U.S. at 317-572-3993, or fax 317-572-4002.

For technical support, please visit www.wiley.com/techsupport.

Wiley also publishes its books in a variety of electronic formats and by print-on-demand. Some content that appears in standard print versions of this book may not be available in other formats. For more information about Wiley products, visit us at www.wiley.com.

ISBN: 978-1-118-30673-4; 978-1-118-30672-7 (ebk); 978-1-118-30674-1 (ebk); 978-1-118-30677-2 (ebk)

Manufactured in the United States of America

10 9 8 7 6 5 4 3 2 1

Publisher's Acknowledgments

Senior Project Editor: Alissa Schwipps

Composition Services: Indianapolis Composition Services Department

Cover Photo: ©iStockphoto.com/Cary Westfall

Special Help: Jenny Brown

WILEY

Table of Contents

● ●

Introduction **1**

About This Book 1

    Foolish Assumptions.. 2

    Icons Used in This Book 2

    Where to Go from Here.. 3

Chapter 1: Welcome to a Mad Great Game **5**

    Breaking Down a Typical Course 6

    Getting Started.. 7

    Playing a Smart Game 8

    Knowing the Critical Rules 10

Chapter 2: Choosing Your Weapons Wisely **11**

    How Much Is This Gonna Cost?................................. 12

        The upscale approach 12

        Golf on a budget.. 13

    Golf Balls: The Dimple Derby 13

    Clubs: Getting Into the Swing................................... 15

        Choosing clubs to put in your bag 16

        Deciding when to use each club 18

    Putting Yourself in Stitches...................................... 19

    Accessories: Getting the Goods................................ 21

    Knowledge is Power: Investing in Lessons.............. 22

Chapter 3: Where to Play and How to Fit In **25**

    Exploring Golf-Course Options 25

        Driving ranges 26

        Public courses.. 27

        Country clubs... 28

        Resort courses 30

    Getting a Deal on Memberships or Green Fees 31

        Making the club scene affordable............................ 31

Saving at resorts and public courses.....................32
Fitting In on the Course 33
When you're the weak link 34
When you're not the worst player..........................35
Avoiding Playing with a Jerk (And Coping
If It Happens Anyway) 36

Chapter 4: Getting Into the Swing.................37

Understanding Swing Basics 37
Building Your Swing...38
Getting a grip...40
Completing the grip..45
Aiming 46
Nailing down the stance 48
Deciding on ball position..49
Amplifying the low point 50
Keeping your eyes on the ball..............................52
Observing the one-hand-away rule......................53
Unleashing Your Swing..54
Making miniswings 54
Testing your rhythm 55
Unwinding...57
Getting yourself together.......................................58
Selecting swing triggers 60
Visualizing shots..61

**Chapter 5: Chipping and Pitching:
Short-Game Secrets.......................................63**

Exploring the Ups and Downs..63
Making Your Pitch...64
Setting Up a Solid Chip 67
Pick your spot 67
Choose the right club...68
Lies and secrets: Considering
your ball placement 68
Chip away! 69

Chapter 6: Putting: The Game within the Game 71

Examining Putters, the Most Important
    Club in the Bag 72
Building Your Putting Stroke 74
    The putting grip 74
    Putting posture: Stand and deliver............................ 79
    Matching your putt to your full swing 82
    Getting up to speed 82
    Reading the break.. 83
    Reading the grain... 84

Chapter 7: Bunker Play: It's Easy (Really!) 87

Throwing Sand: Hitting Bunker Shots............................. 88
Buried Alive! Extracting a Plugged Ball 90

Chapter 8: Rules, Etiquette, and Keeping Score. 93

Playing by the Rules.. 93
    Teeing up 94
    Finding a lost ball.. 95
    Taking a drop 96
Etiquette: Knowing the Right Way to Play 97
Keeping Score 101
    Deciding which format you should play.............. 102
    Comparing match play and stroke play.............. 103
    Getting a handle on the handicap system 105
    Dealing with penalty shots 107

Chapter 9: Solving Common Problems. 111

Respecting the Mental Game 112
    Fear can be your friend... 112
    Proving yourself to yourself..................................... 112
    Positivity... 113
Giving Yourself the Best Shot: Preparing
    for Each Round... 113
    Loosening up... 114
    Warming up your swing... 115

Correcting Common Problem Shots 117

Slicing 117

Hooking 119

Popping up your tee shots 121

Suffering from a power outage 122

Shanking 123

Missing too many short putts 124

Weathering the Elements 126

Handling high winds 127

Swingin' in the rain 129

Chapter 10: Golf's Ten Commandments 131

Take Some Golf Lessons 131

Use a Club That Can Get You to the Hole 132

If You Can Putt the Ball, Do It 132

Keep Your Head Fairly Steady 132

Be Kind to the Course 132

Bet Only What You Can Afford to Lose 133

Keep the Ball Low in the Wind 133

Don't Give Lessons to Your Spouse 133

Always Tee It Up at a Tee Box 134

Keep Your Wits 134

Introduction

● ●

*W*hen I started out on the PGA Tour in 1974, I was full of fight and enthusiasm but lacked a basic knowledge of golf-swing mechanics. So I know what it's like to play without knowledge or a solid foundation. Believe me, I'm a lot happier — and having a lot more fun — now that I know what I'm doing.

The reason I'm qualified to help you is that I have made a serious effort to become a student of the game. When I started working on golf telecasts for CBS, I didn't know much about the inner workings of the swing. But my new job forced me to learn. In *Golf For Dummies,* Pocket Edition, I share my knowledge to help put you on track to becoming not just someone who can hit a golf ball but rather a real golfer. You'll soon discover the big difference between the two.

If this is the first golf book you've ever held in your hands, don't worry. I've read more of them than I can count, and this one's a particular favorite. It's up-to-date with this fast-changing game, and everything is clear and easy to follow. Not to mention funny! Because golf, like life itself, can be hard but is ultimately enjoyable. Please remember that as you begin your adventure in the most maddening and wondrous game of all: Golf is fun. And the fun starts here.

About This Book

I've written this book for the rankest beginner, although I like to think that I have something to offer golfers at every level, even the pros.

What you have here is no ordinary golf-instruction book. Most of the golf books you find in your local bookstore (or, increasingly, online) are written by professional players or teachers. As such, they focus solely on the golf swing. *Golf For Dummies,* Pocket Edition, covers a lot more than the swing. It leads you through the process of becoming a golfer. Beginners need many questions answered as they take on the game. I've organized this book so that you take those steps one at a time and can flip to them anytime for quick reference. May this journey be a pleasant one!

Foolish Assumptions

Because you picked up this book, I assume that you're interested in golf. I also assume that you're not already a great golfer, or else you'd be out there making millions on the PGA Tour. Beyond that, I'm going to figure that you may have dabbled with golf and want to get better. In my experience, most people give golf a try before they seek instruction. It must be an ego thing, kind of like those people who don't like to ask for directions when they get lost because they feel that it's an admission of failure. If that's you, think of me as your personal GPS: your Golfer Positioning System.

Icons Used in This Book

As I guide you through this maze of golf wit and wisdom, I use several handy road signs. Look for these friendly icons; they point you toward valuable advice and hazards to watch out for.

This icon marks golf hazards to avoid or at least be aware of. Be careful!

 This icon flags quick, easy ways to improve your game.

 When you see this icon, be on the lookout for recommendations I swear by (follow them or I will never speak to you again) and important personal stories from my years of playing and covering golf.

 This icon flags information that's important enough to repeat.

Where to Go from Here

Feel free to flip through this book, picking your spots. If you're a complete novice, you may want to take a look at Chapter 1 first. If you're a little more advanced and need help with a specific aspect of your game or swing, you can find that information in Chapters 4 through 7. The rest of the book helps you make that vital jump from "golf novice" to "real golfer."

If you want even more advice on golf, check out the full-size version of *Golf For Dummies* — simply head to your local book seller or go to www.dummies.com.

Chapter 1

Welcome to a Mad Great Game

In This Chapter

▶ Touring a standard golf course

▶ Getting up and swinging

▶ Understanding the benefits of smart play

▶ Following the rules

*Y*ou've probably heard that business leaders are constantly making huge deals on the course, advancing their careers. It's true that golf can help you climb the corporate ladder, but that's only one reason to play.

More-important reasons include spending time with friends, staying in shape, and enjoying some of the most beautiful scenery you'll ever see. Golf is a physical *and* mental challenge; it tests your skill and your will.

Although many rules exist to govern the play of golf, the spirit of the game can be summarized in few words. Simply stated, the goal of golf is to get the ball into each of 18 holes in succession with the fewest number of shots, using no more than 14 clubs. After you hit the ball into all the holes, add up your scores from each hole. The lower your total score, the better. That's it.

Breaking Down a Typical Course

Most golf courses have 18 holes, although a few, usually because of a lack of money or land, have only 9. Courses beside the sea are called *links,* in honor of the parts of Scotland where the game began. (They were the link between beach and farmland.)

Most golf courses are between 5,500 and 7,000 yards. A few are longer, but leave those courses to the pros you see on TV. Start at the low end of that scale and work your way up.

Every hole is a par-3, a par-4, or a par-5. *Par* is the number of strokes a competent golfer should take to play a particular hole. For example, on a par-5 hole, a regulation par may consist of a drive, two more full swings, and two putts.

 Two putts is the standard on every green. Three putts are too many. One putt is a bonus. In a perfect round of par golf, half the allocated strokes should be taken on the greens. That premise makes putting crucial. (I talk about how to putt in Chapter 6.)

With rare exceptions, par-3s are from 100 to 250 yards in length; par-4s are from 251 to 470 yards long, barring severe topography; and par-5s are from 471 to 690 yards. You often find several different teeing areas on each hole so that you can play the hole from different lengths based on your level of skill. Deciding which tee area to use can make you silly. So the tee areas are marked with color-coded tees that indicate ability to help you out:

✔ The **gold tees** are the back tees for long-ball strikers or lower handicap players only.

✔ The **blue tees** are usually slightly ahead of the gold and make the holes shorter, but still plenty hard. Club competitions are played from these tees.

✔ The **white tees** are for everyday, casual play and are the right choice for most men, beginning golfers, and capable senior players. Stray from the white tees at your peril.

✔ The **red tees** are traditionally used by women or junior golfers, although many women I play with use the same tees I play.

Getting Started

If you've never played golf before or otherwise consider yourself a novice, you can easily feel overwhelmed with the many rules and tools that exist, as well as by the thought of hitting a small ball with a small clubhead — or not — without embarrassing yourself in front of more experienced friends or colleagues. Not to worry. Getting started is pretty simple.

1. **Start by picking out golf clubs and balls.**

   You don't have to shell out thousands of dollars to get started. You can start simple — use cheap or borrowed equipment at first, and spend more if you enjoy the game. (Check out Chapter 2 for tips on what you need to get started.)

2. **Know how to grip the club.**

   The *V* between the thumb and forefinger of your top hand should point to your right shoulder (for righties; reverse it if you're left-handed), and the golf club is more in your fingers and not so much in the palm of your hand. (Turn to Chapter 4 for more grip instructions and options.)

3. **Armed with equipment and the right grip, you're ready to swing.**

   Believe me, the swing isn't as easy as it looks. But with practice, you'll get it. (I cover the swing in more detail in Chapter 4.)

Gear, grip, and swing are the barest bones of getting started playing golf. Over time you'll refine your choices and technique as you get to know and improve your game.

Knowing when to hit (and when *not* to), how to keep score, and proper etiquette are integral parts of the game as well. You've probably heard about golf etiquette, handicaps, and one- and two-stroke penalties. If not, don't worry. Chapter 8 gives you the lowdown on these and other important topics.

Playing a Smart Game

Golf's charm lies in the journey. As you play, you find countless ways to get the ball into the hole in as few strokes as possible. Many outside stimuli — and many more inside your head — make golf one of the most interesting, maddening, thrilling, and just plain *fun* endeavors you'll ever find.

The best advice I can give you when you're learning to play, which is just as applicable when you've become a fairly seasoned player, is to relax. Stay calm, make prudent decisions, and never hit a shot while contemplating other matters. You should play golf with complete concentration and no ego.

Also, don't get greedy — play the game one step at a time. Figure 1-1 shows a smart course of action. You start at the tee and hit your drive to Point A. From there, it's 240 yards to the green, with a watery grave lurking to the left. So you lay up to Point B, and go from there to the green via C. This approach doesn't always work — you may *aim* for Point B and still yank your second shot into the pond — but it's the smart play. And that's the key to good golf.

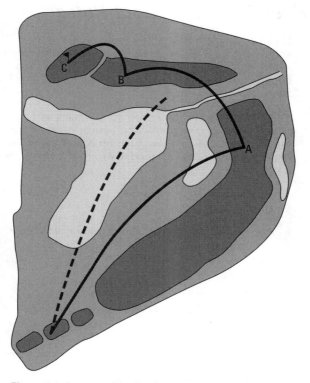

Figure 1-1: A reasonable plan for playing a golf hole.

Score is everything. As you see in Chapters 5, 6, and 7, the most pivotal shots occur within 100 yards of the hole. If you can save strokes there, your score will be lower than that of the player whose sole purpose in life is to crush the ball as far as possible. So practice your putting, sand play, chips, and pitches twice as much as your driving. Your hard work will pay off.

Knowing the Critical Rules

Golf is a game of rules. As with most other sports, some people get giddy about the technicalities. For a smart, enjoyable look at the rules of golf, pick up a copy of *Golf Rules & Etiquette For Dummies* (Wiley) by John Steinbreder.

You also can get by with a few simple rules and a healthy dose of common sense. I cover rules throughout this book and dedicate Chapter 8 to some of the biggies, but you can't go too far wrong on the course if you

- ✔ Play the course as you find it.
- ✔ Play the ball as it lies.
- ✔ Do what's fair if you can't do either of the first two things.

Chapter 2

Choosing Your Weapons Wisely

• •

In This Chapter

▶ Getting a sense of the game's costs

▶ Choosing a golf ball and clubs

▶ Selecting outfits and accessories

▶ Considering lessons

• •

*B*ritain's great prime minister Winston Churchill once griped that golf was "a silly game played with weapons singularly ill-suited to the purpose." Perhaps this was true a hundred years ago, but today's clubs are unrecognizable compared to the rather primitive implements used by the game's early pioneers in the late 19th century.

Early golf equipment certainly had more romantic names — Niblick, brassie, spoon, driving-iron, mashie, and mashie-niblick are more fun than 9-iron, 3-wood, 1-iron, 5-iron, and 7-iron — but today's equipment is much better suited to the purpose of getting the ball down the fairway to the green and then into the hole.

Nowadays, you have no excuse for playing with equipment ill-suited to your swing, body, and game. There's too much information out there to help you. And that's the purpose of this chapter — to help you get started as smoothly as possible.

How Much Is This Gonna Cost?

Take one look at a shiny new driver made of super-lightweight alloys and other space-age materials. Beautiful, isn't it? Now peek at the price tag. Gulp! Each year, the hot new drivers seem to cost a few dollars more — many now retail for $400 and up. And that's just one club. You're going to need 13 more to fill up your golf bag, and the bag itself can set you back another $100 or more. Sure, Bill Gates and Donald Trump are avid golfers, but do you have to be a billionaire to play?

Not at all. Just as you can get a golf ball from the tee into the hole in countless ways, you can get the equipment you need in many ways, too.

The upscale approach

You may be planning to spend thousands of dollars getting started in this game. If so, let me have a word with you: Don't.

Spending doesn't guarantee success. For that, you need a good swing. Still, you can rest assured that if and when you do shell out your hard-earned cash for today's name-brand golf gear, you aren't getting cheated. Golf equipment has never been better suited to its purpose.

Golf on a budget

Getting the most out of today's highest-priced equipment takes a pretty good player. Just as a student driver doesn't need a Maserati to learn the mechanics of driving, beginning golfers can get their games in gear with the golf equivalent of a reliable clunker. If you really keep an eye on costs, you can get started in this game for as little as $100.

Golf Balls: The Dimple Derby

Many technological advances have occurred in golf over the years, but perhaps nothing has changed more than the ball. It's no coincidence that the United States Golf Association (USGA) and the Royal and Ancient Golf Club (R&A) keep a tight rein on just how far a ball can go nowadays. If the associations didn't provide regulations, almost every golf course on the planet would be reduced to a pitch and putt. Everyone would be putting through windmills just to keep the scores up in the 50s.

Even with these regulations, take a look around any golf professional's shop and you see many different brands. And upon closer inspection, you notice that every type of ball falls into one of two categories: Either the manufacturer claims that its ball goes farther and straighter than any other ball in the cosmos, or that its ball gives you more control.

Try not to get overwhelmed. Keep in mind that golf balls come in three basic types: one-piece, two-piece, and three-piece. You can forget one-piece balls — they tend to be cheap and nasty and found only on driving ranges. So that leaves two-piece and three-piece balls.

Don't worry; deciding on a type of ball is still easy. You don't even have to know what a two-piece or three-piece ball contains or why it has that many "pieces." Leave all that to the scientists. And don't fret about launch angle or spin rate either. Today's balls are technological marvels, designed to take off high and spin just enough to go as straight as possible.

 Go with a two-piece ball. I don't recommend a three-piece ball to a beginning golfer. Tour pros and expert players use such balls to maximize control. But as a beginner, you simply need a reliable, durable ball.

Unless you have very deep pockets, go the surlyn, two-piece route. Most beginners use this type of ball. *Surlyn* is a type of plastic, the same stuff covering bowling pins. Assuming you don't whack them off the premises, they last longer than alternatives. They just may roll farther, too.

Golf balls used to come in three compressions: 80, 90, or 100. The 80-compression ball was the softest, and the 100 the hardest. When I was growing up, I thought that the harder the ball, the farther it would go. Not the case. All balls go far when hit properly, but each one feels a little different. Your ideal compression is a matter of personal preference.

 Here's a rule of thumb: If you hit the ball low and want to hit it higher, switch to a softer cover. Your drives will spin more and soar toward the stratosphere. If you hit the ball too high, switch to a ball labeled "low-trajectory."

 Take all the commercial hype with a grain (make that a bowl) of salt. The most important factors you need to know when buying golf balls are your own game, tendencies, and needs. Your local PGA professional can help you choose the golf ball best suited to you.

Virtual pro shops: buying golf gear online

Cyberspace offers a plethora of great pro shops. Every major manufacturer (and even some unusual minor ones) has a presence on the Web, so don't hesitate to check out such sites as `CallawayGolf.com`, `NikeGolf.com`, `Ping.com`, `TaylorMadeGolf.com`, and `Titleist.com`. The following sites specialize in bringing you good prices on brand-name new and used products.

- ✔ **eBay:** At eBay's golf section (`shop.ebay.com/Golf`), you find not only tons of golf balls and clubs (often at great prices) but also clothing, carts, games, and memorabilia — not to mention golf-themed humidors, candles, hip flasks, and plenty of other stuff you never knew existed.

- ✔ **Dick's Sporting Goods:** Visit `Dickssportinggoods.com` and click on the *GOLF* tab for a vast array of golf gear, much of it at bargain prices.

- ✔ **GolfDiscount.com:** For more than 30 years, `GolfDiscount.com` has helped golfers buy top-brand equipment at low prices.

- ✔ **Edwin Watts Golf:** `Edwinwatts.com` offers deals on all sorts of golf gear, including high-quality used clubs.

Clubs: Getting Into the Swing

In the early centuries of golf, players could carry as many clubs as they liked. Since 1938, however, 14 clubs has been the limit. Your collection can include any combination of the following variety of clubs:

✔ **Driver:** The *driver*, the big-headed club with the longest shaft, is what you use to drive the ball off the tee on all but the shortest holes.

✔ **Woods:** *Woods* are lofted clubs (*loft* is the angle at which a clubface is angled upward) that got their names because they used to have wooden clubheads. These clubs are numbered, from the 2-wood and 3-wood up to more-lofted 9- and even 11-woods. Today almost all woods have steel or titanium heads.

✔ **Irons:** *Irons* are generally more lofted than most woods; you most commonly use them to hit shots from the fairway or rough to the green. These include *wedges* for hitting high shots from fairway, *rough* (long grass), or sand.

✔ **Hybrids:** *Hybrids,* sometimes called *utility* or *rescue* clubs, are like a cross between a wood and an iron.

✔ **Putter:** Use a *putter* to roll the ball into the hole.

Choosing clubs to put in your bag

Deciding which clubs to put in your golf bag can be as simple or as complicated as you want to make it. You can go to any store, pick a set of clubs off the shelf, and then take them to the tee. You can pick up a set of clubs at a garage sale or order clubs online. You can also check with the pro at your local municipal course for club recommendations. Any or all of these methods can work. But your chances of using these options and getting a set with the correct loft, lie, size of grip, and all the other stuff involved in club fitting are worse than my chances of winning on *Dancing with the Stars*.

 Having said that, if you're just starting out in golf, you may discover that this game isn't for you. So you should start with rental clubs at a driving range. Most driving ranges rent clubs for a few dollars apiece. Go out and test-wield these weapons to get a feel for what you need.

You're in your experimental stage, so try all sorts of clubs — ones with steel shafts, graphite shafts (which are lighter and therefore easier to swing), big-headed clubs, *investment-cast clubs* (made by pouring hot metal into a mold), *forged clubs* (made from a single piece of metal), and *cavity-backed clubs* (ones that are hollowed out in the back of the iron). You have more choices than your neighborhood Baskin-Robbins.

Don't be afraid to ask your friends if you can try their clubs on the range. I do it all the time when a new product comes out. Try out the clubs and judge for yourself whether they feel good. If you don't like the club you just tried, don't tell the person who loaned it to you that the club stinks — that's not good golf etiquette. Simply hand the club back and say thanks.

After you've swung rental clubs for a while, find cheap clubs to use as an interim set during your adjustment period. You're learning the game, so you don't want to make big decisions about what type of clubs to buy yet. If you keep your ears open around the golf course or driving range, you may hear of someone who has a set that he or she is willing to sell. You can also ask whether people have any information on clubs that you can get cheaply. And, of course, you can check the Internet — the fastest-growing marketplace in golf.

Buy cheap for now but pay close attention to proper length and weight of the golf club. Women and juniors should beware of swinging clubs made for men, which may be too long or too heavy for them. That only makes golf more frustrating! Juniors should start out with junior clubs, women with women's clubs.

When you get a set that fits you and you're hitting the ball with consistency, stick with that set. Finding a whole set of clubs that matches the temperament of your golf swing is hard. Find the ones that have your fingerprints on them and stick with 'em.

Deciding when to use each club

Table 2-1 shows how far the average golfer generally hits with each club when he or she makes solid contact. When you start to play this game, you probably won't attain these yardages, but as you practice, you'll get closer.

The best way to find out your average is to hit, oh, 50 balls with each club. Eliminate the longest five and the shortest five and then pace off to the middle of the remaining group. That's your average yardage. Use this information to figure out which club to use on each shot.

Table 2-1	Which Club Should You Use?	
Club	*Men's Average Distance*	*Women's Average Distance*
Driver	230 yards	200 yards
3-wood	210 yards	180 yards
2-iron	190 yards	Not recommended; 4-wood or hybrid = 170 yards
3-iron	180 yards	Not recommended; 5-wood or hybrid = 160 yards
4-iron	170 yards	150 yards (Consider a hybrid instead)

Club	Men's Average Distance	Women's Average Distance
5-iron	160 yards	140 yards
6-iron	150 yards	130 yards
7-iron	140 yards	120 yards
8-iron	130 yards	110 yards
9-iron	120 yards	100 yards
Pitching wedge	110 yards	90 yards
Sand wedge	90 yards	80 yards
Lob wedge	65 yards	60 yards

Putting Yourself in Stitches

The easiest way to date a photograph of a golfer, at least approximately, is by the clothes he or she is wearing. Sartorially, the game has changed enormously since the Scots tottered around the old links wearing jackets, shirts, and ties.

Fabrics also have changed from those days of heavy wool and restricted swings. Light cotton is what the splendidly smart golfer wears today — if he or she hasn't switched to one of the new, high-tech fabrics that wick perspiration away from the body. (I always said golf was no sweat.)

For today's golfer, it's important to

✔ **Dress within your budget:** This game can get expensive enough; you don't need to out-dress your playing partners. My general rule is to aim to dress better than the *starter* at the course (the person in charge of getting everyone off the first tee). The starter's style is usually a reflection of the dress standards at that particular golf course. If you're unsure about the style at a particular course, give the pro shop a call to find out the dress code.

✔ **Dress comfortably for the season:** If you live in an all-seasons climate and prefer to enjoy the changing weather without giving up your golf game, you need to dress appropriately. For example, in the spring and fall take along extras such as rain gear, a light jacket, and hand warmers because the weather can change faster than you can swing. In the summer add a hat that covers your ears to keep them from getting sunburned. Winterize your game by wearing layers including comfortable long johns and thick socks.

Golf shoes are the final aspect of a golfer's ensemble. Shoes can be a fashion statement in alligator or ostrich. They can be comfortable — tennis shoes or sandals with spikes. They can take on the lore of the Wild West in the form of cowboy boots with spikes or, as my mentor Fairway Louie used to demonstrate, they can even be military combat boots.

What's on the bottom of the shoe is all the rage now. Except for a few top tour pros who swing so hard they need help from their shoes to stay anchored to the ground, everyone plays in *soft spikes*. Soft spikes reduce spike marks and wear and tear on the greens. They're also easier on the feet. If the style of shoes is worthy, you can even go directly from the golf course to the nearest restaurant without changing shoes. The golf world is becoming a simpler place to live.

Accessories: Getting the Goods

When it comes to accessories, you can find a whole subculture out there. By accessories, I mean things such as

- Plastic covers for your irons

- Plastic tubes that you put in your bag to keep your shafts from clanging together

- Tripod tees to use when the ground is hard, or "brush" tees to aid your drive's aerodynamics

- Telescoping ball retrievers to scoop your lost ball from a water hazard

- Rubber suction cups that allow you to lift your ball from the hole without bending down

I've even seen a plastic clip that fits to the side of your bag so that you can "find" your putter quickly. You know the sort of things. Most accessories appear to be good ideas when you purchase them, but then you use them only once.

 The place to find this sort of stuff is in the back of golf magazines. But take my advice: Don't bother. Real golfers don't go for tchotchkes. Accessories are very uncool. The best golf bags contain only the bare essentials:

- About six balls

- A few wooden tees

- A couple of gloves

- A rain suit

- A pitch-mark repair tool

- A few small coins (preferably foreign) for markers

✔ Two or three pencils

✔ A little bag (leather is cool) for your wallet, money clip, loose change, car keys, rings, cell-phone (turned off!), and so on

Your bag should also have a towel (a real, full-size one) hanging from the strap. Use your towel to dry off and clean your clubheads. Keep a spare towel in your bag. If it rains, you can't have too many towels.

One accessory that won't get you laughed off the course is headcovers. Keep them only on your woods or metal woods.

As for your golf bag, you don't need a large tour-sized monstrosity with your name on the side. Especially if you're going to be carrying your bag, go small and get a stand bag — the kind with legs that fold down automatically to support the bag. That way your bag stays on its feet, even on hot August days when you feel like collapsing.

Knowledge is Power: Investing in Lessons

If you just started to play golf and think you may actually want to learn the game, where do you go for help?

✔ **You can get instruction from friends.** Most golfers start out this way, which is why they develop so many swing faults. Friends' intentions are good, but their teaching abilities may not be.

✔ **You can learn by hitting balls.** I learned to play this way. I'd go to the driving range and hit balls day and night. The pure act of swinging a golf club in a certain way made the ball fly in different trajectories and curves. This process is a very slow one because you have to learn by trial and error.

✔ **You can study books.** Many books on golf can lead you through the fundamentals of the game. But you can go only so far by teaching yourself from a book.

✔ **You can take lessons from a PGA professional.** This is the most expensive and most efficient way to learn the game of golf. Lessons can cost as little as $8 an hour and as much as $300 or more. The expensive guys are the ones you read about in *Golf Digest* and *Golf Magazine* and see on TV. But any golf professional can help you with the basics of the game.

Lessons are important. Faults left to fester and boil soon become ingrained into your method. When that happens, curing them can become a lengthy, expensive process. The old adage comes to mind: "Pay me now, or pay me later." Pay your pro early, when your woes are easier to fix.

Golf lessons are available almost anywhere balls are hit and golf is played: driving ranges, public courses, resorts, private clubs, and so on. Just keep in mind that the price of lessons usually increases in that order.

When you do begin working with an instructor, be sure to ask how you can customize an exercise routine to help you get in shape to play better golf. The motivation here is to get you out of the chair where you watch the Golf Channel and into a program that helps you feel better, hit the ball farther, and run circles around your kids. Well, the last one may be a stretch, but the rest is real golf gospel. Here are five areas to address:

✔ Balance
✔ Control

- Flexibility
- Posture
- Strength

If you're deficient in any of these areas, you may develop bad habits in your golf swing to compensate.

Find a specialist to work with and make sure that the exercise program is golf-specific and personalized. A program that isn't designed around your own physical weaknesses, tailored to the special demands of golf, and formulated to accomplish your own performance goals is probably not going to do much to help your golf game.

Chapter 3

Where to Play and How to Fit In

In This Chapter
▶ Playing golf at different kinds of courses
▶ Finding bargains on memberships or green fees
▶ Joining a favorable golf foursome

Golfers play in three main settings: public facilities, private country clubs, and resort courses. In this chapter, I tell you the basics about all three (as well as driving ranges). I also share tips on how to fit in wherever you play — how to walk, talk, tip, dress, and accessorize like a *real* golfer.

Exploring Golf-Course Options

Start with the basics: Where in the world can you play golf?

Some courses have only 9 holes, while a few resorts offer half a dozen — or more! — 18-hole courses. At the famous Pinehurst Resort in North Carolina, you can find eight great 18-hole layouts, including Pinehurst No. 2, one of the finest in the world. China's gigantic

Mission Hills Golf Club, the world's largest, features a full dozen courses — that's 216 chances to drive yourself nuts!

You can also hit balls at driving ranges, which is how you should start, and gradually work up to a par-3 course, building your skills and confidence before you play a regulation 18-hole course. If you rush to the nearest course for your first try at golf, tee off, and then spend most of the next few hours missing the ball, you won't have much fun or be very popular with your fellow golfers. Believe me, they'd rather enjoy a cool beverage in the clubhouse than watch you move large clumps of earth with every swing.

Driving ranges

Driving ranges are basically large fields stretching as far as 400 yards in length. Driving ranges are fun. You can make all the mistakes you want. You can miss the ball, slice it, duff it, top it — do anything. The only people who know are the ones next to you, and they're probably making the same mistakes.

Because driving ranges are often quite long, you can swing for the fences. But you don't have to use your driver. Any good driving range has signs marking off 50 yards, 100 yards, 150 yards, and so on. You can practice hitting to these targets with any club.

Many driving ranges lend or rent clubs, though some expect you to bring your own. As for balls, you purchase bucketfuls for a few dollars — how *many* dollars depends on where you are. In some parts of the United States, you can still hit a bucket of balls for a dollar. But other places, such as Chelsea Piers Golf Club in New York City, charge a lot more.

Public courses

As you'd expect from the name, public courses are open to anyone who can afford the *green fee,* the cost to play a round of golf. Public courses tend to be busy, especially on weekends and holidays. At premier public courses like New York's Bethpage Black, the site of the 2009 U.S. Open, some golfers sleep in their cars overnight so they can be first in line for a tee time the next morning.

Green fees

The cost of a green fee depends on the course and its location. Some humble rural courses charge as little as $10 — and you pay on the honor system, dropping your money into a box! The best public courses can be hard to get on, and they aren't cheap, but most players will tell you they're worth the effort and expense. Upscale public facilities charge $100 and up.

Tee-time policies

Each course has its own tee-time rules. Many let you book a time weeks in advance. Others follow a strange rule: You must show up at a designated time midweek to sign up for weekend play. And some courses you can't book at all — you just show up and take your chance (hence, the overnights in cars). My advice is simple: Phone ahead and find out what the policy is at the course you want to play.

I'm here! Now what?

You've jumped through whatever hoops are necessary to establish a tee time and you know when you're supposed to play. So you pull into the parking lot about an hour before your tee time — to stretch and warm up before you play. What next? Most courses feature a clubhouse. You may want to stop inside to change clothes and buy something to eat or drink.

By all means, make use of the clubhouse, but don't change your shoes in there. If you're already dressed to hit the greens, put on your golf shoes in the parking lot. Then throw your street shoes into the trunk. Don't worry about looking goofy as you lace those spikes with your foot on the car bumper. It's a golf tradition!

The first thing to do at the clubhouse is to find the pro shop. Confirm your time with the pro or *starter* (the person sending groups off from the first tee), and then pay for your round. The pro is sure to be in one of two places: teaching on the practice range or hanging out in the pro shop. If the pro doesn't collect your money, the starter adjacent to the first tee usually does.

After the financial formalities are out of the way, hit some balls on the driving range to warm up those creaky joints of yours. You might also want to go to the putting green and practice short shots. (Chapter 5 covers these shots.)

 Make sure that you're allowed to pitch to the practice green on your course — some courses prohibit it.

Country clubs

In your early days as a golfer, you probably won't play much at country clubs. If you *do* play at a country club — maybe a friend who's a member invites you — it can be intimidating! But don't panic. You're still playing golf; the "goal posts" have just shifted slightly.

 To avoid committing any social faux pas, remember a few club formalities:

✔ **Before you leave home, make sure you're wearing the right clothes.** Wear a shirt with a collar and, if shorts are allowed, go for the

tailored variety that stops just short of your
knees. When in doubt, call the club and ask
about the dress code.

✔ **Get good directions to your destination.** A
stressful journey full of wrong turns doesn't do
your heart rate or your golf game any good.

✔ **Time your arrival so that you have just an hour
to spare before you tee off.** When you drive your
car up the road toward the clubhouse, don't
make the simple mistake of turning sharply into
the parking lot. Go to the clubhouse. Look for a
sign that reads "Bag Drop." A person is no doubt
waiting to greet you. Acknowledge the cheery
hello as if you're doing something you do every
day. Tell him who you're playing with (the club
member who's hosting you). Then get out of your
car, pop the trunk, remove your spikes and hand
him your keys. Tip him a few bucks (or a $5 bill
at a fancy club like Trump International), and
stroll into the clubhouse.

Don't worry about your car or your clubs. The
car will be parked for you, and the clubs will be
loaded onto a golf cart or handed to a caddie.

✔ **Don't try to pay for your round.** Most country
clubs won't take your money. The club member
who's hosting you signs for everything except
tips and pro-shop merchandise. Of course,
you're free to settle up with him or her on your
own — that's between the two of you.

✔ **Once you're inside the clubhouse, head for the
locker room.** Drop off your street shoes next to
your host's locker and then ask for directions to
the bar or to wherever your host is waiting. Don't
offer to buy your host a drink. Members usually
sign tabs and get billed at the end of the month.

✔ **If you have a caddie, remember that he or
she is there to help you.** Trust your caddie's
advice — he or she knows the course better

than you do. Caddie fees at fancy clubs average about $50, which is added to your green fee. You should tip your caddie half the caddie fee at the end of the round, so that's another $25. (Savvy golfers sometimes tip the caddie master before a round; slipping him a $10 bill can get you the best caddie he's got.)

✔ **On the course, be yourself.** And don't worry about shooting the best round of golf you've ever played. Your host doesn't expect that. Even if you happen to play badly, he won't be too bothered as long as you look like you're having fun and keep trying. Just don't complain or make excuses. Nobody likes a whiner.

✔ **After your round, your clubs will probably disappear again, but don't worry: They'll be waiting at the bag drop when you finish your post-round beverage.** Don't forget to tip the bag handlers. Again, a few bucks is usually fine, but be generous if your clubs have been cleaned.

✔ **When you change back into your street shoes, you'll often find them newly polished — that means another few dollars to tip the locker-room attendant.** And when you leave, your golf shoes will have been done, too. Aren't country clubs grand?

✔ **One more tip to go: Give a few bucks to the person who delivers your car back to you and loads your clubs into the trunk.**

Resort courses

You're on vacation, and you're dying to play golf. Where to go? To a resort course, of course.

The great thing about resort courses is that you don't have to be a member — or even have one in tow — to play. The only problem arises when you aren't staying in the right place. Some courses are for certain hotel guests only. And again, prices vary, depending on the course and its location. Generally, though, resort courses cost a good deal more than public courses.

 Phone ahead of time to find out when you can play.

Resort courses are a lot like public courses, but some have bag handlers and other employees who expect to be tipped. Follow the country club tipping guidelines described in the preceding section.

You probably have to rent a cart, too. Carts are mandatory at most resort golf courses. So enjoy the ride! You can drive to your drive and then hop back behind the wheel and putt-putt to your putt.

Getting a Deal on Memberships or Green Fees

Back in the go-go 1990s, hardly anyone thought to ask, "Can I get a discount on country-club membership?" That'd be like asking for a free air-freshener in a new Lamborghini. But times change, and when the economy slows down, prices of upscale items like club memberships and resort-course green fees sometimes come down, too. That can work to your advantage. In the following sections, I give you some insight into scoring deals on playing golf.

Making the club scene affordable

The game's most elite clubs never seem to suffer. You don't see members complaining about the cost of belonging to Augusta National, where pros play the Masters every spring and joining may set you back a cool million. But at other clubs, tough times bring opportunity. Several years ago, many clubs reduced initiation fees from $5,000, $10,000, or even more to nothing to attract new members who'd presumably keep coming back for decades. That's right — you could join for free, as long as you paid your monthly dues of a few hundred dollars.

You see, country clubs rely on much more than upfront fees. They need to sell clubs, balls, and shirts in the pro shop; burgers in the grill room; and drinks in the bar. Their caddies need bags to carry.

And this area is one in which golf, which is often seen as the preserve of old white men, may be changing for the better. Many clubs are more eager than ever to welcome younger, minority, and female players. So if you're thinking of joining a country club, shop around, and don't be afraid to ask whether you can get reduced or waived initiation fees.

Saving at resorts and public courses

The same belt-tightening that squeezes country clubs hits golf resorts and high-end public courses, too. So when you call to arrange a tee time, don't hesitate to haggle. You may say, "I'm bringing two foursomes. Can you give us a price break?" Or, "I'd love to play there, but your green fees are a little high for me."

Asking (politely) never hurts. Even if the answer is no, you can ask for a recommendation on a nice course that's more affordable. You may find a hidden gem.

Also keep in mind that most public facilities and resorts offer *twilight rates*. Tee off in the late afternoon and pay half to two-thirds the usual green fee. Even if you don't finish before dark, you enjoy a course you may want to play again.

Fitting In on the Course

It all starts at the first tee. If you're playing with friends, you don't need any help from me. You know them, and they know you.

That's not the case if you show up looking for a game. If you're at a public course and you've asked the starter to squeeze you in (a few bucks in the starter's hand may get you going sooner rather than later), tell the starter your skill level — and be honest. If you're a beginner, you don't want to be thrown in with three expert players; you'll feel intimidated, probably won't enjoy the round, and likely slow the pace of play.

Golf, like life, has its share of snobs. And some of the worst are single-digit handicappers. Most of them have no interest in playing with a mere beginner. It's a fact of golfing life. Golfers are more comfortable playing with their "own kind." Watch a few groups play off the first tee, and you soon spot a trend. Almost every foursome consists of four players of relatively equal ability. That happens because no one wants to be the weak link in the chain, and no one wants to play with "hackers who can't keep up."

So say the starter groups you with Gary, Jack, and Arnold. Introduce yourself calmly but quickly. Tell them what you normally shoot, if they ask, and make it clear that you're a relatively new golfer. This fact is impossible to conceal, so don't try. But save any additional information, because most golfers really don't care about your game. They make polite noises after your shots, but that's the extent of their interest. You'll soon be that way, too.

Nothing — *nothing* — is more boring than listening to tales about someone else's round. Of course, golf stories are endless, and most are embellished, but they're best used for bonding over beers in the club-house bar, which is also called the *19th hole*.

 Beginners sometimes do things that mark them as misfits on the course. Avoid these blunders at all costs:

✔ **Don't carry one of those telescoping ball retrievers in your bag.** It suggests that you're planning to hit balls in the water.

✔ **Don't wear your golf cap backward.** Ever. No exceptions.

✔ **Don't stretch on the first tee.** Find a place a few yards away, where you don't look like you're auditioning for *The Biggest Loser*.

✔ **Don't dawdle; when it's your turn, be ready!**

When you're the weak link

Early in your golfing existence, almost everyone is better than you. So you'll probably spend some rounds as the worst player in your foursome. What do you do? This section gives you some survival tips.

Pick it up!

The worst thing you can do is delay your playing part-ners. After you've hit the ball, oh, nine times on a given hole, pick it up and quit that hole as a courtesy to your playing partners. There's always the next hole.

Find your own ball

If you happen to hit a shot into the highest spinach patch on the course, don't let your companions help you look for it. Tell them to play on and that you'll catch up after a "quick look." They'll see you as some-one who, though having a bad day, is worth playing

with again. (If you don't find the ball within a few minutes, declare it lost, and put an *X* on your scorecard
for that hole.)

Never moan, never analyze

Most golfers gripe and moan when they're playing
poorly. That's bad — and boring for the other players, who only care that you're slowing things up. So
grit your teeth and keep moving.

Analyzing your swing is another common crime: You
hit a few bad shots — okay, more than a few — then
start talking through your possible corrections. Don't.
I repeat: *Your playing partners don't care about your
game.* So don't analyze, and don't ask them for swing
tips. If one is offered, try it, but keep it quiet.

When you're not the worst player

 How do you behave when another golfer in your
group can't get the ball above shin height? Here
are some pointers:

- ✔ **Zip that lip.** Whatever you do, don't try to
  encourage your pal as his or her game implodes.
  After a while, you run out of things to say, and
  your friend gets annoyed with you.

- ✔ **Never give advice or swing tips.** The other
  person will only blame you for the next bad shot
  he or she hits.

- ✔ **Talk about other stuff.** The last thing you should
  discuss is your pal's awful game. Find some
  common interest and chat about that. Try football, movies, or the stock market. Even politics
  and religion are safer topics than that 20-yard
  drive your friend just dribbled off the tee.

Avoiding Playing with a Jerk (And Coping If It Happens Anyway)

As I mention earlier, most foursomes are made up of players of roughly equal ability. That's what you want. In fact, the best scenario is to find three golfers who are just a bit better than you. By trying to keep up with them, you'll probably improve your usual game.

The people you shouldn't be playing with are those who shoot more than 20 shots lower than you on an average day. All someone like that does is depress you, and your slower, less-expert play may irritate him or her. When you get better, playing with them can help you improve.

In general, most golfers are princes — tall, smart, and handsome (with or without handlebar mustaches). But with more than 25 million American golfers out there, you're bound to encounter a few bad apples. Here's how to deal:

- **At first, ignore the jerk.** Play your game and be glad you're only spending a few hours with Golfzilla.

- **If the jerk keeps it up, speak up.** Being firm but polite often works with jerks. Say, "You walked on my putting line — please don't." Or, "You're distracting me by talking on your cellphone."

- **Treat the jerk as a hazard.** If all else fails, think of Golfzilla the way you think of a strong wind or a lousy lie in a bunker. Golf is all about dealing with adversity. If you can keep your wits and make a good swing despite the jerk, you'll be a tougher, better golfer next time out.

Chapter 4

Getting Into the Swing

● ●

In This Chapter

▶ Finding your pivot point

▶ Exploring the components of a solid golf swing

▶ Improving your performance

● ●

*A*s the great golf expert Duke Ellington once said, "It don't mean a thing if you ain't got that swing." You can be the most stylish-looking golfer in the world, swinging the most expensive driver at the most exclusive club, but without a sound, fundamental swing, you're on the A train to nowhere. This chapter helps you get into the swing of golf.

Understanding Swing Basics

What is a golf swing? That's a very good question, and one that has many different answers. In simple terms though, a *golf swing* is a (hopefully) coordinated, balanced movement of the whole body around a fixed pivot point. If you do it correctly, this motion swings the club up, around, and down so that it strikes the ball with an accelerating blow on the center of the clubface. I'm starting to feel dizzy. How about you?

Balance is the key to this whole swing thing. You can't play golf with consistency if at any time during your swing, you fall over. But when your swing consists of a simple pivot around a fixed point, the clubhead strikes the ball on the same downward path and somewhere near the center of the clubface every time. Bingo!

You're probably wondering where this fixed point in your body is. Well, it isn't your head. It's a myth that you must keep your head perfectly still throughout the swing. I don't advise you to try, unless you've got a chiropractor on retainer.

The fixed point in your golf swing should be in the middle of your chest, about three inches below the spot where your collarbones meet, as shown in Figure 4-1. Your swing rotates around that point. If you get that pivot point correct, your head swivels a little bit as you turn back and then through on your shots. If your head moves like Linda Blair's in *The Exorcist*, you may have a career in the circus, but not in golf.

Building Your Swing

To become a golfer, you must master the building blocks of your swing. How do you hold the club so that you can give the ball a good whack? After you have a good grip, how do you align yourself to the target so that the ball goes somewhere near where you aimed? What should your posture look like? And where in the world should the ball be in your stance? Should you look at the ball or somewhere near the sun? This section has the answers.

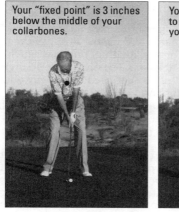

Your "fixed point" is 3 inches below the middle of your collarbones.

Your head swivels to the right as you swing back . . .

then through . . .

all the way to the finish.

Figure 4-1: The proper swing pivot point.

Getting a grip

Although the grip is one of the most important parts of the game, it's also one of the most boring. Few golfers who've played for any length of time pay much attention to hand placement. For one thing, your grip is hard to change after you get used to the way your hands feel on the club. And hand placement simply doesn't seem as important as the swing itself. But that kind of neglect is why you see so many bad grips — particularly among bad players.

Get your grip correct and close to orthodox at the beginning of your golfing career because a bad grip follows you to the grave.

Women tend to have smaller hands than men, so for them, having the right grip size on the club is important. By *grip size,* I mean the width of the rubber (occasionally leather) handle on the club, which is generally smaller for women.

Here's how to sleep well in eternity with the correct grip. Standing upright, let your arms hang naturally by your side. Get someone to place a club in your left hand. All you do now is grab the club and — *voilà!* — you've got your left-hand grip. Well, almost. The grip has three checkpoints:

1. **Place your left thumb and left index finger on the shaft.**

   I like to see a gap of about ¾ of an inch between the thumb and index finger. To get that gap, extend your thumb down the shaft a little. If extending your thumb proves too uncomfortable, pull your thumb in toward your hand. Three-quarters of an inch is only a guide; you have some leeway.

2. **Make sure the grip crosses the base of your last
    three fingers and the middle of your index
    finger, as shown in Figure 4-2.**

    This step is vital. If you grip the club too much in
    the palm, you hinder your ability to hinge your
    wrist and use your hands effectively in the swing.
    More of a finger grip makes it easy to bend the
    wrist on the backswing, hit the ball, and then
    recock the wrist on the follow-through. Just be
    sure that the *V* formed between your thumb and
    forefinger points toward your right ear.

Figure 4-2: Grip more in the fingers of the left hand than in
the palm.

3. **Complete your grip by placing your right hand on the club.**

   You can fit the right hand to the left in one of three ways: the overlapping (or Vardon) grip, the interlocking grip, or the ten-finger grip. I cover each of these grips in the following sections.

Vardon grip

The *Vardon grip* is the most popular grip, certainly among better players. The great British player Harry Vardon, who still holds the record for British Open wins (six) popularized the grip around the turn of the century. Old Harry was the first to place the little finger of his right hand over the gap between the index and next finger of the left as a prelude to completing his grip, as shown in Figure 4-3. Harry was also the first to put his left thumb on top of the shaft. Previously, players kept their left thumbs wrapped around the grip as if they were holding a baseball bat.

Try the Vardon grip. Close your right hand over the front of the shaft so that the *V* formed between your thumb and forefinger points to your right ear. The fleshy pad at the base of your right thumb should fit snugly over your left thumb. The result should be a feeling of togetherness, your hands working as a unit.

Interlocking grip

The *interlocking grip* is a variation of the Vardon grip. The difference is that the little finger of your right hand and the index finger of the left actually hook together (see Figure 4-4). You may find this grip more comfortable if you have small hands. Many top female and junior players use this grip.

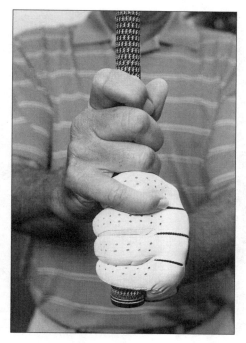

Figure 4-3: In the Vardon grip, the right pinkie overlaps the left index finger.

Ten-finger grip

The *ten-finger grip* is what the name tells you it is. All ten fingers are on the club, like you're gripping a baseball bat. No overlapping or interlocking occurs; the little finger of the right hand and the index finger of the left barely touch (see Figure 4-5).

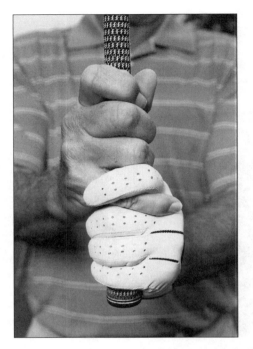

Figure 4-4: Interlock the right pinkie and left index finger if you have small hands.

 If you have trouble generating enough clubhead speed to hit the ball as far as you want, or if you're fighting a slice, give the ten-finger grip a try. This approach can be particularly helpful for female and junior golfers.

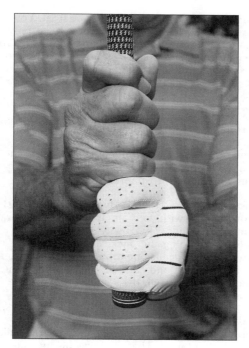

Figure 4-5: You can place all ten fingers on the club in a baseball-style grip.

Completing the grip

Put your right hand on the club, with the palm directly opposite your left hand. Slide your right hand down the shaft until you can complete whatever grip you prefer. Your right shoulder, right hip, and head lean to the right to accommodate the lowering of the right hand. Your right earlobe moves closer to your right shoulder.

Your grip pressure should never be tight. Your grip should be light — no clenching. Exert only as much pressure as you would when picking up an egg from a spotted owl. Lightly now! Spotted owls are becoming extinct!

Aiming

Aiming properly at address is difficult. Generally speaking, right-handed golfers tend to aim too far right of the target and then swing over the top on the way down to get the ball started left. (For help on fixing common faults, see Chapter 9.)

What makes aiming so difficult? Human nature is part of it. Getting sloppy with your aim is easy when your mind is on other things. That's why discipline is important to your golf game. Jack Nicklaus was a great golfer in part because he took the time and trouble to get comfortable and confident in his alignment. He worked his way through the same aiming routine before every shot. And I emphasize *routine*.

First, he'd look at the target from behind the ball. Then he picked out a spot a few feet ahead of his ball on a line with that target. That spot was his intermediate target. Then he walked to the ball and set the clubface behind it so that he was aiming at the intermediate point. Aligning the club with something 2 feet away is much easier than aiming at something 150 yards away.

 Work on your aim to mirror the Nicklaus process and then think of a railroad track. On one rail is the ball and in the distance, the target. On the other rail are your toes. Thus, your body is aligned parallel with — but left of — the target

line. Your feet should be parallel to the target
line, not aimed at the target. If you take nothing
else away from this section on aiming, remember that phrase. Cut out Figure 4-6 and tape it
onto the ceiling over your bed. Stare at it before
you go to sleep.

Figure 4-6: Align your body so your feet are *parallel* to the
target line.

Don't make the mistake that I see countless golfers making: aiming their feet at the target. Think
about it: If you aim your feet at the target, where
is the clubface aligned? To the right of where
you want the ball to go! Instead, get your feet
aligned a little to the left of the target line, *parallel* to it. It'll feel like you're aimed to the left —
that's a *good* thing!

Nine perfect excuses for a bad shot

Try some of these convincing lines the next time your shot doesn't go where you wanted it to:

- ✔ "I only had an hour to loosen up."

- ✔ "I looked up and the sun got in my eyes."

- ✔ "I just had a lesson, and the pro screwed me up."

- ✔ "I borrowed these clubs."

- ✔ "These new shoes are killing my feet."

- ✔ "This new glove cuts off my circulation. I have the hand of a mummy."

- ✔ "I kept expecting your cellphone to go off."

- ✔ "I can't play well when the temperature is over 80. Or under 79."

- ✔ "I'm Gary McCord."

Nailing down the stance

Okay, you're aimed correctly. But your feet aren't finished yet. Right now you're just standing there. All the books tell you to turn your left toe out about 30 degrees. But what's 30 degrees? Think of it this way: Point your left foot to 10 o'clock and your right foot to 1 o'clock. Keep it simple and always be on time.

Width of stance is easy, too. Keep your heels shoulder-width apart, as shown in Figure 4-7. Not 14 inches or 18 inches. Shoulder width. Let the shape of your body dictate the right stance for you.

With a driver, the gap between your knees should be shoulder width. Think "bow-legged."

Figure 4-7: Your knees should be as far apart as your shoulders.

Deciding on ball position

Where is the ball positioned between your feet? When using a driver, you want it aligned with your left armpit (see Figure 4-8). That means the ball is also aligned with your left heel. For other clubs, the ball moves steadily back with each club until you get to the middle of your stance with a wedge.

For a driver, place the ball opposite your left armpit.

Figure 4-8: Ball position.

Amplifying the low point

The bottom of the swing is an important, often-neglected aspect of golf. After all, that's usually where the ball is! The arc of the swing has to have a low point; hopefully, that low point is precisely where your golf ball is as you swing an iron.

If you don't know where the bottom of your swing is, you don't know where to put the ball in your stance.

You can make the best swing in the world, but if the ball is too far back, you hit the top half of it. Too far forward is just as bad; you hit the ground before the ball.

Fear not; such shots aren't part of your repertoire. Why? Because you always know where the bottom of your swing is: directly below your head.

Think about it. The preceding section discusses how the ball is aligned with your left armpit when you use the driver. That position automatically puts your head behind the ball whenever you swing your driver. In other words, the ball is nearer the target than your head is, which means that you strike the ball a slightly upward blow. The bottom of the swing is behind the ball, so the clubhead is moving up as it hits the ball, as shown in Figure 4-9. That's all right because the ball is perched on a tee. The only way to make solid contact (and maximize your distance) is to hit drives "on the up."

Figure 4-9: Tee the ball about an inch high for an upward strike with the driver.

The situation for an iron shot from the fairway differs from that of the driver. Now the ball is sitting on the ground. Plus the club you're using has more loft and is designed to give best results when the ball is struck just before the ground. So now your head should be over the ball at address and impact. Something has to move.

That something is the ball. Start from the middle of your stance, which is where the ball should be when you're hitting a wedge, one of the shortest and most lofted clubs in your bag. Move the ball steadily forward as the club in your hands gets longer.

Of course, you're not actually physically moving the ball until you hit it. What's moving in the stance is you — your setup in relation to the ball.

Keeping your eyes on the ball

I see too many players address the ball with their chins on their chests (probably because other golfers have said, "Keep your head down!"). Or, if they've been warned not to do that, they hold their heads so high they can barely see the ball. Neither, of course, is exactly conducive to good play.

So how do you position your head? The answer is in your eyes. Look down at the ball, which is in what optometrists call your *gaze center*. Your gaze center is about the size of a Frisbee. Everything outside your gaze center is in your peripheral vision.

Now lift or drop your head slightly. As your head moves, so do your eyes, and so does the ball — into your peripheral vision. Suddenly, you can't see the ball so well. But if you hold your head steady enough to keep the ball inside that Frisbee-shaped circle, you can't go too far wrong. Try to keep the ball in the middle of your gaze center.

Observing the one-hand-away rule

One last thing on address position: Let your arms hang so that the *butt* end of the club (the one with the handle) is one hand-width from the inside of your left thigh, as shown in Figure 4-10. Use this position for every club in the bag except your putter.

The club should be one hand from your body.

The shaft of a wedge should point at the crease in your left pant leg (or the middle of your thigh).

A driver should point at your zipper.

Figure 4-10: Your hands and the club.

The butt end of the club is a useful guide to check the relationship between your hands and the clubhead. With a wedge, for example, the butt end of the club should be in line with the middle of your left thigh. For a driver, it should be opposite your zipper. Every other club is between those parameters.

Unleashing Your Swing

Now it's time to do what you've been wanting to do: Create some turbulence. Many people think the most effective way to develop a consistent swing is to stand on the range whacking balls until you get it right. But the best way to develop a consistent swing is to break the swing down into pieces. Only after you have the first piece mastered do you move on to the next one. In the sections that follow, I deal with each part of the swing and cover a few other considerations, too.

Making miniswings

I start the swing process with what I call *miniswings*. Position yourself in front of the ball as I describe in "Building Your Swing" earlier in this chapter. Now, without moving anything but your hands, wrists, and forearms, rotate the club back until the shaft is horizontal to the ground and the *toe* of the club (the part of the clubhead farthest from the shaft) is pointing up.

The key to this movement is the left hand, which must stay in the space that it's now occupying, its address position (see Figure 4-11). The left hand is the fulcrum around which the swing rotates. The butt of the club should stay in about the same position while your hands lift the clubhead.

From address, push down with your left hand as you pull up with your right.

Rotate the club back until the shaft is horizontal, the toe pointing up.

Figure 4-11: The miniswing.

After you get the hang of that little drill, try hitting shots with your miniswing. Let the club travel through 180 degrees, with the shaft parallel to the ground on the backswing and then back to parallel on the through-swing; your follow-through should be a mirror image of the backswing. The ball obviously doesn't go far with this drill, but your hands and arms are doing exactly what you want them to do on a full swing: Cock the wrists, hit the ball, and recock the wrists.

After you have the miniswing down, you can turn on the horsepower and get your body involved.

Testing your rhythm

One of the most effective ways for your brain to master something like the golf swing is to set the motion to music. Music plays a valuable role

in the learning process. You learned your ABCs
by putting the letters to song. So when you start
to move the club and your body into the swing,
think of a melody. Make the song real music.
The golf swing should be a smooth motion, so
your song should reflect that smoothness. Think
Tony Bennett, not Eminem. I've played some of
my best golf while humming Hootie and the
Blowfish tunes.

To begin adding body movement to your miniswing
motion (see the preceding section), stand as if at
address, with your arms crossed over your chest so
that your right hand is on your left shoulder and your
left hand is on your right shoulder. Hold a club
against your chest with both hands, as shown in
Figure 4-12a.

Figure 4-12: Turn your body.

Now turn as if you're making a backswing (see Figure 4-12b). Turn so that the shaft turns through 90 degrees, to the point where it's perpendicular to a line formed by the tips of your toes. As you do so, let your left knee move inward so that it points to the golf ball. The butt of the club also points at the ball.

The key here is keeping your right leg flexed. The only way to get the shaft into position is by turning your body. You can't sway or slide to the right and still create that 90-degree angle.

 Your backswing should feel as if you're turning around the inside of your right leg until your back faces the target. That's the perfect top-of-the-backswing position.

Unwinding

From the top, let your body unwind back to the ball in the proper sequence. (Your spine angle must stay the same from address to the top of the backswing.)

Uncoiling starts from the ground up. The first thing to move is your left knee. That knee must shift toward the target until your kneecap is over the middle of your left foot, where it stops. Any more shifting of the knee, and your legs start to slide past the ball. An *alignment stick* (a flexible fiberglass stick used to help with alignment) poked into the ground just outside your left foot is a good check that your knee shift hasn't gone too far. (See the top left photo in Figure 4-13.) If your left knee touches the stick, stop and try again.

Next, your left hip slides targetward until it's over your knee and foot. Again, a stick in the ground provides a good test — a deterrent to keep your hip from going too far.

Pay special attention to the clubshaft across your chest in this phase of the swing (work in front of a mirror if you can). The shaft should always parallel the slope of your shoulders as you work your body back to the ball.

Swing through the impact area all the way to the finish. Keep your left leg straight and let your right knee touch your left knee, as shown in the bottom photo in Figure 4-13. Hold this position until the ball hits the ground — that way, you prove beyond doubt that you've swung in balance.

Getting yourself together

Practice the exercises in the preceding sections. All together, they comprise the basis of a pretty sound golf swing that combines hands/arms and body motion.

1. **Practice your miniswing.**

2. **Hum a mellow tune.**

3. **Turn your shoulders so that your back is toward the target.**

4. **Turn, don't slide; sliding automatically takes your head off the ball.**

5. **At the finish, keep your left leg straight, with your right knee touching your left knee.**

Coordinating the parts into a solid golf swing takes time. The action of the parts soon becomes the whole, and you develop a feel for your swing. But knowledge, in this case, doesn't come from reading a book. Only repetition — hitting enough balls to turn this information into muscle memory — can help you go from novice to real golfer. So get out there and start taking some turf!

An alignment stick at address

Bends if you slide forward (wrong)

But not if you turn (nice!)

Figure 4-13: Turn, don't slide.

Selecting swing triggers

The rhythm of your swing should fit your personality. If you're a fairly high-strung, nervous individual, your swing is probably faster than most. If your swing is slower, you may be more laid back and easygoing. But the potential for great rhythm is within every golfer.

Yet good rhythm doesn't just happen. You need to set the tone for your swing with your waggle. A *waggle* is a motion with the wrists in which the hands stay fairly steady over the ball and the clubhead moves back a foot or two, as if starting the swing. (Check one out in Figure 4-14.)

Figure 4-14: Get in motion with a waggle.

Waggling the club serves three main purposes:

> ✔ **It's a rehearsal of the crucial opening segment of the backswing.**
>
> ✔ **It can set the tone for the pace of the swing.** In other words, if you have a short, fast swing, make short, fast waggles. If your swing is of the long and slow variety, make long, slow waggles. Be true to your species.
>
> ✔ **It gives your swing some momentum.** In golf, you don't want to start from a static position. You need a running start to avoid an abrupt, jerky beginning to your swing. Waggling the clubhead eases tension and introduces movement into your setup.

But the waggle is only the second-to-last thing you do before the backswing begins. The last thing is your *swing trigger,* which frees you to get the club away from the ball. A swing trigger can be any kind of move. For example, 1989 British Open champion Mark Calcavecchia shuffles his feet. Gary Player, winner of nine major championships, always kicked his right knee in toward the ball. Your swing trigger is up to you. Create the flow!

Visualizing shots

As you practice your swing and hit more and more shots, patterns — good and bad — emerge. The natural shape of your shots becomes apparent. Few people hit the ball dead-straight; they either *fade* most of their shots (the ball flies from left to right) or *draw* them (the ball moves from right to left in the air). If you hit a ball that curves from left to right, aim far enough left to allow the curve of your ball to match the curve of the hole, and vice versa.

If either tendency gets too severe and develops into a full-blooded slice or hook (a *slice* is a worse fade, and a *hook* is a worse draw), stop playing. Go get a lesson. One session with a pro should get you back on track.

 Don't let your faults fester. They can quickly become ingrained into your method, making it much more painful to correct them.

After you've developed a consistent shot shape that works, you can start to visualize how that shape fits the hole you're playing. Then, of course, you know exactly where to aim — whether the hole is a *dogleg right* (turns right), *dogleg left* (turns left), or straight-away. You're a real golfer.

Chapter 5

Chipping and Pitching: Short-Game Secrets

● ●

In This Chapter

▶ Understanding the short game and its importance

▶ Making pinpoint pitch shots

▶ Chipping your way to great shots

● ●

*F*ive-time PGA champion Walter Hagen had the right approach. As he stood on the first tee, the great Haig knew that he'd probably hit at least six terrible shots that day. So when he did hit one sideways, he didn't blow his top. Hagen simply relied on his superior *short game* (every shot within 80 yards of the hole) to get out of trouble.

Of course, everything within 80 yards of the hole includes putting (which I discuss in Chapter 6) and sand play (Chapter 7). So what's left for this chapter to cover? Pitching and chipping — two versions of short shots to the green.

Exploring the Ups and Downs

Hang around golfers for a while and you inevitably hear one say something like, "I missed the third green but got up and down for my par." At this stage, you're probably wondering what in the world *up and down* means. Well, the *up* part is the subject of this chapter — *chipping* (hitting a low, short shot) or *pitching* (hitting a higher, more airborne short shot) the ball to the hole. The *down* half of the equation is holing the putt after your chip or pitch (see Chapter 6). Thus, a golfer with a good short game is one who gets up and down a high percentage of the time (above 50 percent).

You can make up for a lot of bad play with one good short shot. As someone once said, "Three of them and one of those makes four." Remember that saying; even if you need three cruddy shots to get near the green, you can save par with a nice chip or pitch.

Making Your Pitch

Pitch shots, which you play with only your wedges and 9-iron, are generally longer than chips and stay mostly in the air. That introduces wrist action into the equation, which opens the issue of how long your swing should be and how fast. In other words, pitch shots need some serious feel.

Even the best players try to avoid pitch shots. They're in-between shots. You can't just make your normal, everyday, full swing — that would send the ball way too far. You're stuck making a partial swing — which is never easy, especially when you're under pressure.

Here's how to build your pitching swing.

1. **Set up a narrow stance about 12 inches from heel to heel and open, with your left foot back from the target line.**

   Your shoulders should be open to the target which makes it easier to sense the target and to swing the club back closer to the intended flight

line with your hands ahead of the ball, leading
the clubhead. Stand so that the ball is about two
inches to the left of your right big toe.

2. **Make a miniswing (described in Chapter 4).**

   Without moving the butt end of the club too far
   in your backswing, hinge your wrists so that the
   shaft is horizontal. Now swing through the shot.

3. **Watch how far the ball goes and make
   adjustments.**

   That distance is your point of reference. Do you
   want to hit the next pitch 10 yards farther? Make
   your swing a little bit longer (see Figure 5-1).
   Shorter? Your swing follows suit. That way, your
   rhythm never changes. You want the clubhead
   accelerating smoothly through the ball. And you
   best achieve that acceleration if you build up the
   momentum gradually from *address* (the point
   right before you hit the ball).

Poor pitchers of the ball do one of two things: Either
they start their swings too slowly and then speed up
too much at impact, or they jerk the club away from
the ball and have to decelerate later. Both swings lead
to what golf columnist Peter Dobereiner christened
"sickening knee-high fizzers" — low, thin shots that
hurtle uncontrollably over the green — or complete
duffs that travel only a few feet. Not a pretty sight.
The most common cause of both is tension. So relax!

 Imagine that you're swinging with a potato chip —
the thin, crispy American kind — between your
teeth. Focus on *not* biting down on it. That'll
keep you relaxed.

In golf, you get better by doing, so improve your
pitching by practicing. Here's a game we play at the
back of the range at our facility at Grayhawk Golf Club
in Scottsdale, Arizona. We get five empty buckets and
place them in a straight line at 20, 40, 60, 80, and 100
feet. We then have one hour to hit one ball into each

bucket, starting at 20 feet. The winner gets the title to
the other guy's car. We're still driving our own cars —
we usually get frustrated and quit before the one-hour
time limit expires, or we go to lunch. But at least we
get some good pitching practice.

From address...

swing the club with
hands/arms only...

accelerate
through impact
to a relaxed finish.

Figure 5-1: Achieving the proper momentum.

Last pitching thought: Although pitch shots fly higher than chips, you still want to get the ball back to the ground quickly so that it doesn't sail too far. Pick out your landing area somewhere short of your final target and let the ball roll the rest of the way. See the shot in your mind's eye before you hit the ball, and remember your *Golf For Dummies* secret: To make the ball go up, hit down — don't try to lift it. The loft on the club's face is designed to get the ball airborne.

Setting Up a Solid Chip

Chip shots are shorter than pitches; they stay mostly on the ground. Chips are also easier than pitches, or at least they should be. With the proper technique, you can chip the ball close enough to the hole to tap the ball in . . . unless, of course, you sink that chip!

Chips are played around the greens with anything from a 5-iron to a wedge. (Head to Chapter 2 for the lowdown on these and other clubs.) The basic idea is to get the ball on the green and rolling as soon as you can. If you get the ball running like a putt, you have an easier time judging how far it will go. The following sections point out some vital chipping considerations.

Use the philosophy I outline in these sections as a starting point, not as holy writ that you follow to the letter. Go with your instincts to choose the right club or shot. The more you practice this part of your game, the easier it gets.

Pick your spot

Your first point of reference is the spot where you want the ball to land. If at all possible, you want that spot to be on the putting surface. The turf there is generally flat and well-prepared, which makes the all-important first bounce more predictable. Try to avoid landing chips on rough, uneven, or sloping ground.

Pick a spot about two feet onto the green. From that spot, I like to visualize the ball rolling the rest of the way to the hole. Visualization is a big part of chipping. Try to picture the shot before you hit the ball. Then be as exact as you can with your target. Don't aim for an area. Try to hit a blade of grass! You can't be too precise. For a specific practice exercise, see the later section "Chip away!"

Choose the right club

Your club choice depends on how much room you have between your landing point and the hole. If you have only 15 feet, you need a more *lofted* club (one with a face that's severely angled back from vertical), such as a sand wedge or even a lob wedge, so the ball doesn't run too far. If that gap is bigger (say, 60 feet), a straighter-faced club, such as a 7-iron, is more practical.

Practice, and only practice, makes you better. Try all sorts of clubs for these shots. Sooner or later, you develop a feel for the short game. I can't stress this point enough: Use as many clubs as possible when practicing! Observing how different clubs perform in different situations is one of the secrets of a successful short game.

Lies and secrets: Considering your ball placement

Now consider how your ball is lying on the ground. If it's in long grass, you need to use a more lofted club and make a longer swing, no matter where the hole is.

(**Remember:** Longer grass means a longer swing.) You need to get the ball high enough to escape the rough. If the ball is lying *down* (in a depression) and you can't get it out with a straighter-faced club, you have to go to more loft and move the ball back a little in your stance — closer to your right foot — to make the shot work. This part of the game calls for creativity.

Chip away!

 Short game guru Phil Rodgers taught me my chipping technique, which is basically the same one I employ for putting. I use a putting stroke with a lofted club — and I want you to do the same. Take your putting grip and stroke, and go hit a few chip shots. Right now — unless you're operating heavy machinery.

One key to chipping is your setup. Creating the right position at address is essential. Your stance should be similar to the one you use on pitch shots: narrow, with about 12 inches from heel to heel, and open, with your left foot back from the target line. Your shoulders should be open to the target as well. Now place about 80 percent of your weight on your left side. By moving your hands ahead of the ball, you encourage the downward strike that you need to make solid contact with the ball. The ball should be about 2 inches to the left of your right big toe, as shown in Figure 5-2.

 During your stroke, focus on the back of your left wrist. That wrist must stay flat and firm, as in putting. To keep your left wrist flat, tape a popsicle stick to the back of that wrist (slipping the stick under your watchband works almost as well). You feel any breakdowns right away. Now go hit some putts and chips.

Figure 5-2: Chip with your weight on your left side and your hands ahead of the ball.

Chapter 6

Putting: The Game within the Game

• •

In This Chapter
▶ Choosing a putter
▶ Hitting good long and short putts

• •

*T*he chapters in this book are all my babies — I love
'em each and every one. But this one may be the
most important, because putting skills are vital in golf.

 Statistically, putting is 68 percent of the game of
golf, so you may want to take notes. You'd be
smart to keep a "reminder book" of putting tips,
because you can't score well if you can't putt —
it's that simple.

If you want proof, look at the top professionals on tour
who average about 28 putts per round. In other words,
these professionals are one-putting at least 8 of the 18
greens in a round of golf. The average score on tour
isn't 8 under par, so even these stars are missing their
fair share of greens. And where are they making up for
their mistakes? That's right: on good putts.

Golfers often say they're *rolling the rock* on the green
rather than *rolling the ball*. Don't ask me why. I sus-
pect it has to do with the difficulty of rolling a hard,

irregular object that can hurt you. Or maybe *rock* and *roll* just go together.

No other part of golf induces as much heartache as putting. Many fine strikers of the ball have literally been driven from the sport because they couldn't finish holes as well as they started them. Why? Because putting messes with your internal organs. Every putt has only two possibilities: You either hole it or miss it. Accept that, and you won't have night-mares about the ones that "should" have gone in.

Examining Putters, the Most Important Club in the Bag

Because putting is such a crucial part of golf, your putter is the most important weapon you've got. Club makers seem to have noticed: In recent years, they've brought out a dizzying array of high-tech putters. Some are as sleek as a sports car, while others look more like anvils or spaceships. One new model has been likened to "a fire hydrant on a stick." How can you choose the putter that's best for your game? It's not as tricky as you may think.

Although you have many putters to choose from, you can eliminate most of them by knowing the type of putter you are. In other words, the shape of your stroke is the main factor in choosing a putter. Figure 6-1 shows two types of putters.

My good friend and noted teaching professional Peter Kostis explains that almost all putting strokes fall into one of two shapes. They either move "straight back and straight through" with the blade staying square, or "inside to inside," the blade doing a mini-version of the rotation in a full swing. Conveniently, most putters are designed to suit one of those two stroke shapes. Following are the two main types of putters:

- ✔ Face-balanced, center-shafted putters
- ✔ Putters that aren't face-balanced, such as heel-shafted blades

If keeping the blade square throughout the putting stroke is your style, get a face-balanced, center-shafted model. You can test to see if a putter is face-balanced by resting the shaft on your finger. If the putterface stays parallel to the ground, it's face-balanced. The inside-to-inside stroke is easier to make on a consistent basis with a heel-shafted putter. It hangs toe-down while resting on your finger. (The *toe* is the end of the putter, the part farthest from the shaft.)

Some putters hang at an angle of 45 degrees. They're equally good — or bad! — for either stroke.

Figure 6-1: Which kind of putter do you prefer?

Building Your Putting Stroke

You can putt well using any number of methods or clubs, but at this stage, you should putt in as orthodox a manner as possible. That way, when something goes wrong — which it will — the fault is easier to fix. The trouble with being unorthodox is that finding order in the chaos is more difficult.

The putting grip

The putting grip isn't like the full-swing grip (refer to Chapter 4). The full-swing grip is more in the fingers, which encourages your wrists to hinge and unhinge. Your putting grip's purpose is exactly the opposite.

 Grip the putter more in the palm of your hands to reduce the amount of movement your hands make. Although you may putt well with a lot of wrist action in your stroke, I prefer that you take the wrists out of play as much as possible. Unless you have incredible touch, your wrists aren't very reliable when you need to hit the ball short distances. You're far better off relying on the rocking of your shoulders to create momentum in the putterhead.

Not all putting grips are the same — not even those grips where you place your right hand below the left in conventional fashion. But what almost all putting grips have in common is that the palms of both hands face each other so that your hands can work together. The last thing you want is your hands fighting one another. Both hands need to work together.

In the conventional grip, your hands can work together in one of two ways, as shown in Figure 6-2. Start by placing the palms of your hands on either side of the club's grip. Slide your right hand down a little so that you can place both hands on the club. You should feel like you're going to adopt the ten-finger grip (refer to Chapter 4). Then do one of the following, depending on which grip you prefer:

Place your palms on opposing sides of the grip.

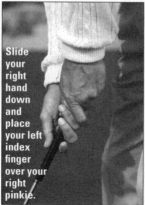

Slide your right hand down and place your left index finger over your right pinkie.

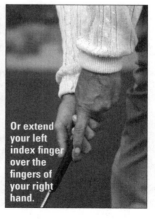

Or extend your left index finger over the fingers of your right hand.

Figure 6-2: A gripping start.

✔ **Place your left index finger over the little finger of your right hand.** This is known as the *reverse overlap*.

✔ **Extend your left index finger past the fingers of your right hand until the tip touches your right index finger.** I call this grip the *extended reverse overlap*. The left index finger, when extended, provides stability to the putting stroke.

Go with the grip that feels most comfortable. I describe other ways to grip the putter in the following sections.

Left hand low

This method is commonly referred to as *cross-handed*. The left hand hangs below the right with the putter (or vice versa if you're a lefty). Many players use this method because it helps keep the lead hand (the left, in this case) from bending at the wrist as you hit the ball. (See Figure 6-3.)

One of the biggest causes of missed putts is the breakdown of the left wrist through impact. When the left wrist bends, the putter blade twists. This twisting causes the ball to wobble off-line, no matter what kind of fancy putter you use. That's why you want to maintain the bend of your left wrist from the address position all the way through the stroke.

Another reason you see many of today's pros using a cross-handed grip is that, with the left arm lower on the shaft, you pull the left shoulder more square to your target line. Pulling your left shoulder happens automatically with this grip. I tend to open my shoulders (aim to the left) with my putter. As soon as I tried a cross-handed grip, my left shoulder moved toward the target line, and I was squarer to my line.

A left-hand-below-right putting grip helps stop left-wrist breakdown.

Figure 6-3: Keep that left wrist firm.

GARY SAYS

I think the left-hand-low method's best asset is that you swing the left arm back and forth during the stroke. The trailing hand (right) goes along for the ride, which is a great way to stroke your golf ball. I suggest that you try putting with

your left hand low. You may stick with this
method forever.

The claw

To try the claw, start with a standard putting grip.
Turn your right palm toward you and bring it to the
putter's handle so that the handle touches the spot
between your thumb and index finger. Now bring
your index and middle fingers to the shaft, leaving
your ring finger and pinkie off, as shown in Figure 6-4.

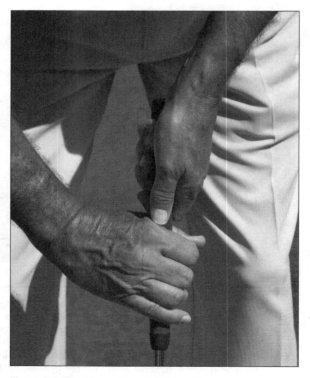

Figure 6-4: The claw grip — another option.

Putting posture: Stand and deliver

As you crouch over the ball to putt, your knees should flex slightly. If your knees are locked, you're straining your back too much. Don't bend those knees too much, though, or you may start to look like a golf geek!

Bend from your waist so that your arms hang straight down. This position allows your arms to swing back and forth from a fixed point in a pendulum motion. Hold your arms straight out from your body. Bend down with those arms outstretched from the waist until your arms are pointing to the ground. Now flex your knees a little, and you're in the correct putting posture.

You can break a lot of rules in how you stand to hit a putt (see Figure 6-5). Ben Crenshaw, one of the best putters ever, always stood open to the target line, his left foot drawn back. Gary Player did the opposite: He set up closed, his right foot farther from the target line than his left. But that's their style; I keep things simple with a square stance so that I don't need to make many in-stroke adjustments to compensate.

Toeing the line

As in a full swing, the line of your toes is the key to good putting posture. Regardless of which stance you choose, your toe line should always be parallel to your target line. Be aware that the target line isn't always a straight line from the ball to the hole — if only putting were that simple! Few greens are flat, so putts *break* or bend from right to left or from left to right. So sometimes you aim a few inches to the right of the hole, and other times maybe a foot to the left. Whatever you decide, your toe line must be parallel to your target line.

On breaking putts, aim your feet parallel to the line you've chosen, not toward the hole. In effect, you make every putt straight. Applying a curve to your putts is way too complicated and affects your stroke. Imagine how you'd have to adjust if you aimed at the hole and then tried to push the ball out to the right because of a slope on the green. You'd have no way to be consistent.

To putt, you can stand open. Or closed. Or square.

Figure 6-5: Putting stances vary.

Standing just right

Okay, now what about width of stance? Again, you have margin for error, but your heels need to be about shoulder-width apart at address.

You have to bend over to place the putter behind the ball. How far should you bend? Just far enough to get your *eye line* (the direction of your gaze — a much-neglected part of putting) directly over the ball.

 To find that position, place a ball on your forehead between your eyes, bend over, and let the ball drop, as shown in Figure 6-6. Where does the ball hit the ground? That's where the ball should be in relation to your body. It shouldn't be to the inside, the outside, behind, or in front of that point. It should be right there, dead center. This alignment places your eyes not just over the ball but also over the line that you want the ball to ride.

Drop the ball from a point between your eyes.

Where the ball lands is where it should be positioned in your stance.

Figure 6-6: Your eyes should be over the ball.

Matching your putt to your full swing

One basic rule for a beginning golfer is to match the length of your golf swing to your putting stroke. That is, if you have a *short swing* (your left arm, if you're right-handed, doesn't get too far up in the air on your backswing), make sure that your putting stroke is a short one, too. If your full swing is *long,* make your putting stroke long. This way, you're consistent.

Your swing tells a lot about your personality. If your golf swing is long and slow, you're probably an easy-going person. If your swing is short and fast, you're probably the type who walks around with his hair on fire.

Getting up to speed

In my decades in pro golf, I've seen players of all shapes and sizes with a lot of different putting methods. Some putted in what could be termed mysterious ways, and others were totally conventional. So analyzing different putting methods is no help. The best way to look at putting is to break it down to its simplest level. The hole. The ball. The ball fits into the hole. Now get the ball into the hole in the fewest possible strokes.

You want to get the ball rolling at the right speed. That means hitting a putt so that if the ball misses the cup, it finishes 14 to 18 inches past the hole. This distance is true no matter the length of the putt. Two feet or 40 feet, your aim must be to hit the ball at a pace that has it finish 14 to 18 inches beyond the hole. If it doesn't go in, that is.

A putt can't possibly go in if you don't get it to the hole.

You're probably wondering why your ball needs the right speed. Well, the right speed gives the ball the greatest chance of going into the hole. Think about it: If the ball rolls toward the middle of the cup, you don't want it moving so fast that it rolls right over the hole. If it touches either side of the cup, it may drop in. Your goal is to give the ball every chance to drop in, from any angle — front, back, or side.

The only putts that *never* drop are the ones you leave short of the hole. If you've played golf for any length of time, you've heard the phrase "never up, never in." The cliché is annoying but true. As the Irish say, "Ninety-nine percent of all putts that come up short don't go in, and the other 1 percent never get there." Remember that! Also remember that you should try to sink every putt from 10 feet or closer. I *hope* to make every putt from 10 to 20 feet, and I try to get every putt close from 20 feet and beyond.

Reading the break

After you have the distance control that a consistent pace brings, you can work on the second half of the putting equation: reading the break. The *break* is the amount a putt moves from right to left, or left to right. Slope, the grain of the grass, topographical features such as water and mountains, and, perhaps most important, how hard you hit the ball dictate the break. For example, if I'm an aggressive player who routinely hits putts several feet past the cup, I'm not going to play as much break as you do. (***Remember:*** You want to hit your putts only 14 to 18 inches past the cup.)

The firmer you hit a putt, the less the ball breaks on even the steepest gradient. So don't be fooled into thinking that you can hole a putt one way only. On, say, a 20-footer, you probably have about five possibilities. How hard you hit the ball is one factor.

The first thing I do when I arrive at a golf course is to find the natural slope of the terrain. If the course is near mountains, finding the natural slope is easy. Say the mountains are off to the right on the first hole. Any slope on that hole runs from right to left. In fact, the slope on every green is going to be "from" the mountain (unless, of course, a particularly humorless architect has decided to bank some holes toward the mountain). So I take that into account on every putt.

If the course is relatively flat, go find the pro or course superintendent. Ask about nearby reservoirs or, failing that, the area's lowest point. This point can be 5 miles away or 20 — it doesn't matter. Find out where that point is and take advantage of gravity. Gravity is a wonderful concept. Every putt breaks down a hill — high point to low point — unless you're in a zero-gravity environment. But that's another book.

After you know the lowest point, look at each green in detail. If you're on an older course, the greens probably slope from back to front to aid drainage. Greens nowadays have more humps and undulations than ever and are surrounded by more bunkers. And the sand tells a tale: Most courses are designed so that water runs past a bunker and not into it. Take that insight into account when you line up a putt. And don't forget the barometric pressure and dew point — just kidding!

Reading the grain

Golf is played on different grasses (ideally, not on the same course). Climate usually dictates the kind of grass you find on a course. When dealing with grasses, architects try to use the thinnest possible blade, given the climate, and then try to get that grass to grow straight up to eliminate grain.

Grasses in hot, tropical areas have to be more resil-
ient, so they typically have thick blades. *Bermuda
grass* is the most common. Its blades tend to follow
the sun from morning to afternoon — in other words,
from east to west. Because the blade is so strong,
Bermuda grass can carry a golf ball according to the
direction in which it lies. Putts *downgrain* (with the
grain) go faster than putts *into* (against) the grain. All
that, of course, has an effect on your putt.

 Look at the cup to find out which way the
Bermuda grass is growing. Especially in the afternoon, you may see a ragged half and a smooth, or
sharp, half on the lip of the cup — that shows the
direction in which the grass is growing. The
ragged look is caused by the grass's tendency to
grow and fray. If you can't tell either way, go to
the *fringe* (the edge of the green). The grass on
the fringe is longer, so you can usually see the
direction of the grain right away. The grain of the
fringe is the same as on the green.

Another common type of grass is *bent grass.* You see
this strain mostly in the northern and northeastern
United States. Bent grass has a thinner blade than
Bermuda grass, but it doesn't stand up to excessive
heat as well.

Bent grass is used by many golf-course builders
because it allows them to make the greens fast, and
the recent trend for greens is to combine slope with
speed. Try getting on the roof of your car, putting a
ball down to the hood ornament, and making it stop.
That's how slippery greens with bent grass can feel.

 I don't concern myself much with grain on bent
greens. Bent is better than Bermuda when it
comes to growing straight, so grain is rarely a
factor on bent greens. I just worry about the
slope and the 47 things on my checklist before I
putt. Putting could be so much fun if I didn't
have a brain.

Chapter 7

Bunker Play: It's Easy (Really!)

- -

In This Chapter
▶ Understanding sand play
▶ Making sand shots easy
▶ Dealing with a less-than-perfect lie

- -

I've read countless articles and books on sand play, and they all say the same thing: Because you don't even have to hit the ball, playing from the sand is the easiest part of golf. Well, I say that's bull trap! If sand play were so easy, all those articles and books would never be written in the first place. Everyone would be blasting the ball onto the putting green with nary a care in the world. And take it from me, that's not the case.

In this chapter, I explain the techniques you need to get out of the sand. I even tell how to hit a successful bunker shot from a terrible lie. Do *that* your next time out and your friends will be amazed.

Bunkers, or sand traps (as I'm told *not* to call them), provoke an extraordinary amount of "sand angst" among golfers. But sometimes, *aiming* for a bunker actually makes sense — on a long, difficult approach shot, for example. The pros know that the *up and down* (getting onto the green and then into the hole) from sand can actually be easier than from the surrounding (usually gnarly) grass.

Throwing Sand: Hitting Bunker Shots

Okay, you're in a greenside bunker. You want to get the ball onto the putting surface. Here's what to do:

1. **Open your stance by pulling your left foot back until you start to feel vaguely ridiculous.**

   Your left foot's position must feel funny to you. If it doesn't, pull your foot back even more!

2. **Open (turn to the right) your sand wedge until the face points almost straight up at the sky, as shown in Figure 7-1.**

   Make sure you position the ball forward in your stance toward your left heel. (The ball should be even farther forward if you're unlucky enough to be very close to the face of the bunker.) You should feel like the club will slide right under the ball when you swing at it — and this position should feel just as weird as your wide-open stance. Again, if it doesn't, open the face of your sand wedge even more.

   Take advantage of your sand wedge. This club works best when the face is wide open (turned clockwise). Sand wedges are designed so that the open face sends the ball up when you slide it into the sand.

3. **Aim about a credit-card length (about 3¼ inches) behind the ball and swing at about 80 percent of full speed.**

   Use a sliding motion. Don't hit down. Let the clubhead throw a scoop of sand onto the green.

Figure 7-1: Open your stance and wedge face until they feel ridiculous.

Focusing on a full, uninhibited follow-through helps. Forget the ball; all you want to do is throw sand out of the bunker; the ball gets carried along for the ride. And that's why better players say that bunker play is easy — the clubhead never actually contacts the ball. (*Remember:* The more sand you throw, the shorter the shot is. So if you need to hit the shot a fair distance, hit maybe only two inches behind the ball.)

Remember that your club must not touch the sand before you hit the ball. That's *grounding* the club — illegal in a hazard.

Buried Alive! Extracting a Plugged Ball

Unfortunately, not every *lie* (where the ball is sitting) in a bunker is perfect. Sometimes the ball *plugs,* or embeds itself in the sand so that only part of it is visible. Some golfers call this lie a *fried egg,* but don't reach for a spatula. Instead, after you're through cursing your bad luck, try a different technique.

To exhume your ball from a buried lie, follow these steps:

1. **Set up your stance and clubface.**

   You need to open your stance as you do for any sand shot (see the preceding section). But this time, don't open the clubface. Keep it a little *hooded.* In other words, align the clubface to the left of your target. Shift nearly all your weight to your left side, which puts you ahead of the shot, and play the ball back in your stance. This situation is the one time you *want* the leading edge of the club to dig. The ball, after all, is below the surface of the sand.

2. Swing the club up and down.

And I mean *up* and *down* like you're chopping wood with a dull ax. Hit straight down on the sand a couple of inches behind the ball as shown in Figure 7-2. A follow-through isn't necessary. Just hit down. Hard. The ball should pop up and then run to the hole. With little or no backspin, that sneaky little escapee runs like it just stole something. So allow for extra roll.

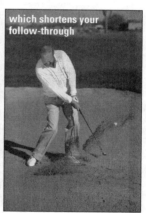

Figure 7-2: Hit down hard to excavate a plugged ball.

Just how hard you should hit down is difficult for me to say — it depends on the texture and depth of the sand and on how deep the ball is buried. That old standby, practice, is a terrific guide.

Second-to-last point: Practice with clubs of various lofts, and then use whatever works for you. I often use my pitching wedge (which has less bounce and a sharper leading edge than a sand wedge, and there-fore digs more) for buried-lie escapes. (See the side-bar "Gotta bounce: Exploring how a club's bounce affects sand shots" for more on bounce.)

Last point: Always smooth out your footprints when leaving a bunker — that's golf etiquette. If no rake is nearby, use your feet.

Gotta bounce: Exploring how a club's bounce affects sand shots

To be a competent sand player, you must take advantage of the way your sand wedge is designed. The bottom of the club is wider than the top. The *bounce* is the part of a wedge that hangs below the *leading edge*, the front part of the *sole*. (The sole, like the bottom of a shoe, is the bottom of the clubhead.) Believe me, if you can make the best use of the bounce, you have nothing to fear in sand play.

The bounce is the part of the clubhead that should contact the sand first. This approach encourages the sliding motion that's so crucial to good play in bunkers. Think about it: The sand is going to slow the club as you swing down and through, which is okay. But you want to keep the slowdown to a minimum. If the club digs in too much, the ball probably won't leave the bunker. So *slide* the clubhead; don't use it to dig.

Not every sand wedge has the same amount of bounce. The width of the sole and the amount that it hangs below the leading edge varies. The lower the *trailing edge* (the rear part of the sole) hangs below the leading edge, the more bounce your sand wedge has.

How do you know how much bounce your sand wedge needs? The determining factor is the type of sand you play from. The bigger the bounce or the wider the sole on your sand wedge, the less the wedge digs into the sand.

If the sand at your home course is typically pretty firm underfoot, you need a sand wedge with very little bounce. At the other end of the scale is soft, deep sand. For that sort of stuff, you need plenty of bounce. In fact, because the clubhead digs so easily when the sand is soft, you can't have enough bounce in those bunkers.

Chapter 8

Rules, Etiquette, and Keeping Score

* *

In This Chapter

▶ Knowing the rules

▶ Respecting other golfers

▶ Scoring the game

* *

Golf is a beautifully structured game, rife with rules of play, etiquette, and scoring that have evolved through its long history. You don't have to memorize all 182 pages of the United States Golf Association's latest *Rules of Golf*, but you must know the essentials, and this chapter gives you the run-down on them.

Playing by the Rules

Take a look at a rulebook today (you can pick one up from almost any professional's shop, or order one directly from the USGA), and you find a seemingly endless list of clauses and sub-clauses — all of which make the game sound very difficult and complicated.

In my opinion, the Rules are too complex. For a smart, enjoyable look at them, pick up a copy of *Golf Rules & Etiquette For Dummies* (Wiley) by John Steinbreder.

In the meantime, you can't go too far wrong if you observe the following three guidelines:

- ✔ Play the course as you find it.
- ✔ Play the ball as it lies.
- ✔ Do what's fair if you can't do either of the first two things.

Teeing up

You must tee up between the markers — not in front of them and no more than two club lengths behind them (see Figure 8-1). If you tee off outside this area — also called the *tee box* — you get a two-shot penalty in stroke play; in match play, you must replay your shot from the teeing area. (See the "Comparing match play and stroke play" section later in this chapter for more on these two kinds of golf games.)

You don't have to tee up your ball right between the markers; you can go back as much as two club lengths.

Figure 8-1: The tee box is bigger than you think.

You don't have to stand within the teeing area; your feet can be outside it. This knowledge is helpful when the only piece of level ground is outside the teeing area or if the hole is a sharp dogleg. You can give yourself a better angle by *teeing up wide* (standing outside the teeing area).

Finding a lost ball

At this stage of your golf life, you're going to hit your share of errant shots. Some will finish in spots where finding a deer, bear, or Keebler elf seems easier than locating your golf ball. And sometimes you can't find the ball at all.

You have five minutes to track down your ball. Time yourself. If you can't find the ball in the five minutes you're allowed, you must return to the tee or to the point where you last hit the ball and play another ball. With penalty, stroke, and distance, you're now hitting off the tee with three strokes under your belt. (The later section "Out-of-bounds" gives you more details on penalty, stroke, and distance.)

 One way to avoid having to walk back to the tee after failing to find your ball is to hit a provisional ball if you think the first one may be hard to find. If the first ball can't be found, you play the second.

Be sure, however, to announce to your playing partners that you're playing a provisional ball. If you don't, you must play the second ball — *with* the penalty — even if you find the first ball.

Ain't this game full of surprises?

 Looking for a ball is a much-neglected art form. I see people wandering aimlessly, going over the same spot time after time. Be systematic! Walk back and forth without retracing your steps. That's how search parties work.

Taking a drop

In some situations, you have to pick up your ball and drop it. Every golf course has places that allow you to take a free drop. A cart path is one — you can move your ball away from the path with no penalty. *Casual water* (such as a puddle) is another. Here's how to drop your ball:

1. **Lift and clean the ball.**

2. **Find the nearest spot where you have complete relief from the problem and mark that spot with a tee.**

   You have to get not only the ball but also your feet away from the obstruction, so find a spot where your feet are clear of the obstruction, and then determine where the clubhead would be if you hit from there. This is the spot you want to mark. The spot you choose can't be closer to the hole.

3. **Measure one club length from that mark.**

4. **Drop the ball.**

   Stand tall, holding the ball at shoulder height and at arm's length. Let the ball drop vertically. You aren't allowed to spin the ball into a more favorable spot. Make sure the ball doesn't end up nearer the hole than it was when you picked it up. If it does, pick up the ball and drop it again.

How you drop the ball makes no difference; however, you always have to stand upright when dropping. I once had to drop my ball in a bunker where the sand was wet. The ball was obviously going to *plug* when it landed (that is, get buried in the sand), so I asked whether I could lie down to drop it. A clever idea, I thought — but totally wrong. The answer was no.

Etiquette: Knowing the Right Way to Play

Golf, unlike the trash-talking sports you see on TV, still prizes sportsmanship. Golf is an easy game to cheat at, so every player is on his or her honor. But there's more to it than that. Golf has its own code of etiquette: semiofficial "rules" of courtesy that every player is expected to follow. Here are the main ones:

✔ **Don't talk while someone is playing a stroke.** Give your partners time and silence while they're analyzing the situation, making their practice swings, and then making their swings for real. Don't stand near an active player or move about either, especially on the greens. Stay out of another player's peripheral vision during a putt. Don't stand near the hole or walk between your partner's ball and the hole. Even be mindful of your shadow. The *line* of a putt — the path it must follow to the hole — is holy ground.

Easygoing types may not mind if you gab away while they're choosing a club, but that isn't true for everyone. When in doubt, stand still and shut up. If you're a problem more than once, expect to hear about it.

✔ **Be ready when it's your turn — when your ball lies farthest from the hole.** Make your decisions while you're walking to your ball or while waiting for others to hit. And when it's your turn, don't delay. You don't have to rush; just get on with it.

✔ **The *honor* (that is, the first shot) on a given tee goes to the player with the lowest score on the previous hole.** If that hole was tied, the player with the lowest score on the hole before that retains the honor. In other words, you have the honor until you lose it.

✔ **Make sure everyone in your foursome is behind you when you hit.** You don't hit every shot where you're aiming it. When in doubt, wait for your playing partners to get out of your line of play. The same is true for the group in front; wait until they're well out of range before you hit. Even if it would take a career shot for you to reach them, hold your fire.

✔ **Pay attention to the group behind you, too.** Are they waiting for you on every shot? Is there a gap between you and the group ahead of you? If the answer to either or both is yes, step aside and invite the group behind you to play through. This move is no reflection on your ability. All it means is that the group behind plays faster than you do.

The best place to let a group behind play through is at a par-3 (it's the shortest hole and, therefore, the quickest way of playing through). After hitting your ball onto the green, mark it, and wave to them to play. Stand off to the side of the green as they hit. After they've all hit, replace your ball and putt out. Then wait for them to finish, and let them go to the next tee ahead of you. Simple, isn't it?

✔ **Help out the greenskeeper.** A busy course takes a major pounding — all those balls landing on greens, feet walking through bunkers, and divots of earth flying through the air. Do your bit for the golf course. Repair any ball marks you see on the greens. (You can use your tee or a special tool called a *divot fixer,* which costs about a dollar in the pro shop.)

Here's how to repair ball marks:

1. **Stick the repair tool in the green around the perimeter of the indentation, starting at the rear, and gently lift the compacted dirt.**

2. **Replace any loose pieces of grass or turf in the center of the hole and then take your putter and tap down the raised turf until it's level again (see Figure 8-2).**

   Now you're a good golf citizen.

   You also want to smooth out or rake any foot-prints in bunkers, as shown in Figure 8-3 (but only after you play out). And replace any divots you find on fairways and tees.

✔ **If you must play with a golf cart (my advice is to walk if you can), park it well away from greens, tees, and bunkers.** To speed up play, park on the side of the green nearest the next tee. The same is true if you're carrying your bag: Don't set the bag down near any of the afore-mentioned items; leave it in a spot on the way to the next tee.

✔ **Leave the green as soon as everyone has fin-ished putting.** You see this situation a lot: You're ready to play your approach shot to the green, and the people in front are crowding around the hole marking their cards. That's poor etiquette on two counts: It delays play, and the last thing the greenskeeper wants is a lot of footprints around the cup. Mark your card on the way to the next tee!

When a ball lands on a soft green, it often leaves a *pitch mark*.

Lift the back edge of the hole...

and then flatten it out.

Figure 8-2: Take care of the green.

Figure 8-3: Be rakish and restore the bunker.

Keeping Score

Scoring is another unique part of golf. You can easily see how you're doing because your score is in black and white on the scorecard. Every course has a score-card that tells you each hole's length, its par, and its rating relative to the other holes (see Figure 8-4).

The relationship of the holes is important when you're playing a head-to-head match. Say I have to give you 11 shots over 18 holes because of our handicap difference (check out the section "Getting a handle on the handi-cap system" for more on handicap). In other words, on 11 holes during our round, you get to subtract one shot from your score. The obvious question is, "Which holes?" The card answers that question. You get your shots on the holes rated 1 through 11. These holes, in the opinion of the club committee, are the hardest 11 holes on the course. The 1-rated hole is the toughest, and the 18-rated hole is the easiest.

Most of your golf will typically be matches against others. That's why each hole's rating is important.

Don't get too wrapped up in how many shots you're taking to play a round though, at least at first. For many golfers, the score doesn't mean that much anyway. Most of the guys I grew up with never kept score. That's because they were always playing a match against another player or team. In a match like that, all that mat-ters is how you compare with your opponents. It's never "me against the course"; it's always "me against you." So if I'm having a really bad hole, I simply concede it to you and then move on to the next one.

That's a totally different game from the one that you see the pros playing on TV every week. For them, every shot is vital — the difference between finishing in or out of the big money. That's why the pro game is better left to the pros.

Men's Course Rating/Slope Blue 73.1/137 White 71.0/130													Women's Course Rating/Slope Red 73.7/128		
Blue Tees	White Tees	Par	Hcp	PAUL	JOHN	NICK	JERRY	HOLE					Hcp	Par	Red Tees
377	361	4	11	5	4	6	3	1					13	4	310
514	467	5	13	4	7	6	5	2					3	5	428
446	423	4	1	5	5	5	5	3					1	4	389
376	356	4	5	4	5	5	4	4					11	4	325
362	344	4	7	5	4	4	3	5					7	4	316
376	360	4	9	4	6	5	5	6					9	4	335
166	130	3	17	4	2	3	3	7					17	3	108
429	407	4	3	4	5	6	5	8					5	4	368
161	145	3	15	3	4	4	4	9					15	3	122
3207	2993	35		38	42	44	37	Out						35	2701
Initial													**Initial**		
366	348	4	18	4	4	5	4	10					14	4	320
570	537	5	10	6	5	5	7	11					2	5	504
438	420	4	2	5	4	6	4	12					6	4	389
197	182	3	12	4	4	5	4	13					16	3	145
507	475	5	14	5	5	4	5	14					4	5	425
398	380	4	4	6	5	4	6	15					8	4	350
380	366	4	6	4	4	5	4	16					10	4	339
165	151	3	16	3	3	4	3	17					18	3	133
397	375	4	8	3	4	6	5	18					12	4	341
3418	3234	36		40	38	44	42	In						36	2946
6625	6227	71		78	80	88	79	Tot						71	5647
Handicap				14	15	18	11						Handicap		
Net Score				64	65	70	68						Net Score		
Adjust													Adjust		

Paul Sipp	*Jerry Tottla*	8-9-10
Scorer	Attested	Date

Figure 8-4: A sample scorecard.

Deciding which format you should play

GARY SAYS

The best format I know of for the beginning golfer is a *scramble*. In that format, you're usually part of a team of four. Everyone tees off, and then everyone plays another shot from where the best shot lies. And so on. A scramble is great for beginners because you have less pressure to hit every shot well. You can lean on your partners a bit. Plus, you get to watch better players up close. And you get to experience some of the game's camaraderie. Scrambles are typically full of rooting, cheering, and high-fives. In short, they're fun.

You can also play in games where the format is *stableford.* In this game, the scoring is by points rather than strokes. You get one point for a *bogey* (score of one over par); two for a par; three for a *birdie* (one under par); and four for an *eagle* (two under par). Thus, a round in which you par every hole reaps you 36 points. The great thing is that in a stableford, you don't have to complete every hole. You can take your 9s and 10s without irreparably damaging your score. You simply don't get any points for a hole in which you take more than a bogey. That's with your handicap strokes deducted, of course.

You may well find that you play most of your golf with three companions. That's known as a *foursome* in the United States (a *four-ball* elsewhere). The format is simple. You split into two teams of two and play what is known as a *best-ball* game. That is, the best score on each team on each hole counts as the score for that team. For example, say we're partners; if you make a 5 on the first hole and I make a 4, our team scores a 4 for the hole.

Comparing match play and stroke play

In *match play,* you don't have to write down any score. The only thing that matters is the state of the game between you and your opponent. The score is recorded as holes up or holes down. In other words, say my score on the first hole was 4, and your score was 5, and you received no strokes on that hole. I'm now one up.

Because each hole is a separate entity, you don't need to write down your actual score; you simply count the number of holes you've won or lost. In fact, if you're having a particularly bad time on a given hole, you can even pick up your ball and concede the hole. All you lose is that hole. Everything starts fresh on the next tee. Such a head-to-head match ends when one player is more holes up than the number of holes remaining. Thus, matches can be won by scores of *four and three.* That means one player was four holes ahead with only three left, the match finishing on the 15th green.

Stroke play (or *medal play*) is different. It's strictly card-and-pencil stuff. Now you're playing against everyone else in the field — or against that elusive standard, par — not just your playing companion. All you do is count one stroke each time you swing at the ball. If it takes you five strokes to play the first hole, you write *5* on your card for that hole.

Well, your opponent does — your playing partner keeps your official score, although you can track it as well if you want. The card in your pocket has your playing companion's name on it. At the end of the round, he signs his name to your card and gives it to you; you do the same with his card. After you've checked your score for each hole, you also sign your card. Then, if you're in an official tournament, you hand your card to the scorers. If you're playing a casual round, you record your score on the computer.

 Take care when checking your card. One Rules of Golf quirk is that you're responsible for the accuracy of the score recorded under your

name for each hole — your companion isn't.
Any mistakes are deemed to have been made by
you, not him. And you can't change a mistake
later, even if you have witnesses.

But don't worry about the math on your card. You
aren't responsible for that part. As long as the numbers
opposite each hole are correct, you're in the clear.

Getting a handle on the handicap system

If you, as a beginner, are completing 18-hole rounds in
fewer than 80 shots, you're either a cheat or the next
Jack Nicklaus. In all probability, your scores are con-
siderably higher than par. Enter the handicap system.

The USGA employs the handicap system to level the
playing field for everyone. The handicap system is
one reason I think that golf is the best of all games.
Theoretically, handicapping allows any two players,
whatever their level of play, to have an enjoyable —
and competitive — game together. The following sections explain how to figure out your handicap and
how it impacts your game.

Getting a handicap

You probably don't have a handicap yet. No worries —
you've got plenty of time. When you can consistently
hit the ball at least 150 yards with a driver, you're
ready to play a full 18-hole round of golf.

The first thing to do is play a round on a real course
and keep score. Get a golfer friend to accompany you
for 18 holes. This person must keep score and sign
your card at the end of the round. To be valid, a card
needs two signatures: your own and that of the
person you're playing with. That way, all scores are
clearly valid, and nobody fudges his or her total.

You need to play at least ten rounds before you're eligible for a handicap. Don't ask why; those are the rules. After ten rounds in a pre-handicap cocoon, you emerge as a beautiful, full-fledged, handicap golfer.

Calculating your handicap

Okay, you're wondering how you get a handicap. It's easy: All you do is report your scores at the course where you normally play. Then you're off and running. Your handicap at any one time is the average of the best 10 of your previous 20 scores. Technically, it's 96 percent of that number — another wacky golf quirk.

Most country clubs and public courses make things easy for you. They have computers that take your scores and do all the work to update your handicap throughout the golf season, about twice a month.

Suppose your ten scores average out at exactly 100. In other words, for your first ten rounds of golf, you hit 1,000 shots. If par for the 18-hole course you played is 72, your average score is 28 over par. That figure, 28, is your handicap.

Every time you play from then on, your handicap adjusts to account for your most recent score. Suppose your 11th round is a 96. That's only 24 over the par of 72. So your *net score* — your actual score minus your handicap — is 68, four under that magic number of 72. Nice round! When you feed that 96 into the handicap computer, you'll likely find that your handicap drops.

Understanding what your handicap means

A low handicap reflects solid golfing skills. Thus, if your handicap is 6 and mine is 10, you're a better player. On average, four strokes better, to be exact.

Assume that par for the 18-hole course we're going to play is 72. You, as someone with a handicap of 6, would be expected to play 18 holes in a total of 78 strokes, six more than par. I, a 10-handicapper, would on a normal day hit the ball 82 times, ten more than par. Your handicap is the number of strokes over par you're expected to take to play an 18-hole course.

 When you're just starting out, you don't want to team up with three low-handicap players — that's just discouraging. Play with golfers of your own ability at first. After you get the hang of the game, start playing with people who are better than you so that you can learn from them.

Putting it on a scorecard

Keeping score with handicaps is simpler than it looks. Say your handicap is 9 and mine is 14. That means you're going to give me five strokes over the course of the round. I get those strokes at the holes rated the most difficult. That's logical. Equally logical is the fact that these holes are handicapped 1 through 5. So mark those "stroke holes" before you begin.

 After the match begins, keep track of the score with simple pluses or minuses in a spare row of boxes.

Dealing with penalty shots

Penalty shots are an unfortunate part of every golfer's life. Sooner or later, you're going to incur a penalty shot or shots. I can't cover all the possible penalty situations in this book, but here are the most common.

Out-of-bounds

Out-of-bounds is the term used when you hit your ball to a spot outside the confines of the golf course — over a boundary fence, for example. Out-of-bounds areas are usually marked with white stakes that are about 30 yards apart and often abbreviated with the dreaded *O.B.* If you're outside that line, you're out-of-bounds.

Okay, so it's happened; you've gone out-of-bounds. What are your options? Limited, I'm afraid. First, you're penalized *stroke and distance.* That means you must drop another ball (or tee up if the shot you hit out-of-bounds was from a tee) as close as possible to the spot you just played from. Say that shot was your first on that hole. Your next shot counts as your third on that hole. Count'em:

- The shot you hit
- The stroke penalty
- The distance

So now you're *playing three* from the original spot.

Unplayable lies

Inevitably, you're going to hit a ball into a spot from which further progress is impossible. In a bush. Against a wall. Even buried in a bunker.

 When the unplayable lie happens (and you're the sole judge of whether you can hit the ball), you have three escape routes.

- You can pick up the ball and drop it — no nearer the hole — within two club lengths (take your driver and place it end-to-end on the ground twice) of the original spot under penalty of one shot.

- You can pick up the ball, walk back as far as you want (keeping that original point between you and the hole), and then drop the ball. Again, it's a one-stroke penalty.

✔ You can return to the point where you hit the original shot. This option is the last resort because you lose distance and add the penalty shot. A long walk while you're burdened with a penalty stroke feels terrible!

Water hazards

Water hazards are intimidating when you have to hit across one. Whenever you see yellow stakes, you know the pond/creek/lake in question is a water hazard. If you hit into a water hazard, you may play the ball as it lies, with no penalty, if the ball's only half-submerged or otherwise hittable. (If you do, you may not *ground your club* — touch it to the ground or water before swinging.) Or you can choose from these options:

✔ Hit another ball from the spot you just hit from.

✔ Take the point where your ball crossed into the water hazard and drop another ball (you can go back as far as you want, keeping that point between you and the hole).

Either way, it's a one-shot penalty.

Lateral water hazards

If you're playing by the seaside, the beach is often termed a *lateral water hazard.* Red stakes indicate a lateral hazard. Your options are to play the ball as it lies (no penalty, but risky) — as with regular water hazards, you may not ground your club — or as follows, with a one-stroke penalty:

✔ Drop a ball at the point where the ball last crossed the boundary of the hazard — within two club lengths, no nearer the hole.

✔ Drop a ball as close as possible to the spot on the opposite margin of the water hazard, the same distance from the hole.

✔ Hit another ball from within two club lengths of the spot you just hit from.

✔ Take the point where the ball crossed the water hazard and drop another ball as far back as you want, keeping that point between you and the hole.

Strike one! The dreaded whiff

It's the beginner's nightmare: You make a mighty swing and miss the ball. The penalty? None, actually. But you must count that swing as a stroke.

If you swing at a ball with intent to hit it, that's a shot, regardless of whether you make contact. You can't say, "That was a practice swing." If you meant to hit the ball, your swing counts as a stroke.

Chapter 9

Solving Common Problems

• •

In This Chapter

▶ Noticing golf's head games

▶ Appreciating the value of preparation

▶ Finding a way out of swing trouble

▶ Taming errant tee shots

▶ Dealing with Mother Nature

• •

*T*he old saying is true in golf, as in life: Nobody's perfect. In golf, nobody's even close. Even the best players have some little hitches in their methods that bedevil them, especially under pressure. Watch your playing companions when they get a little nervous; you can see all sorts of unfortunate events. They leave putts short and take longer to play even simple shots. Conversation all but stops. Any flaws in their swings are cruelly exposed.

No matter how far you progress in this game, you're going to develop faults of your own. They're a given. The trick is catching your faults before they get worse. Faults left unattended often turn into major problems and ruin your game. In this chapter, I cover how to head off (pun intended) the potential negative aspect of golf's mental game and provide a solid warm-up routine. Then I discuss the most common swing faults you're likely to develop, with cures for each one. I also address some ways for dealing with less-than-ideal weather conditions during your game.

Respecting the Mental Game

So many things can go wrong in this game that it's easy to start thinking negatively. Believe me, I've been there, bogeyed that. Even the world's best golfers have days when the club feels like "an instrument ill-suited to the purpose," to quote Winston Churchill. Fortunately, more than 500 years of golf history have provided some tried-and-true ways to cope, and I discuss those in the following sections.

Fear can be your friend

Many golfers feel fear on the course. But you can make fear work for you by turning it into something less scary: caution.

If you're facing a scary shot, stop and think: Can I more safely get to the green? Even if it takes an extra shot, that's better than wasting two or three strokes on failed miracles.

And if you've got no choice but to go for broke, there's no shame in hitting a bad shot if you give it your all.

Proving yourself to yourself

Self-doubt can turn the best golf swing into a mess of flying knees and elbows. How can you beat it? Practice.

That may sound obvious, but too many golfers rely on hope to keep them out of trouble. They say, "I hope this works" and flail away, trying to hook a shot between trees, over a lake to a postage-stamp green. But if you've never hooked a ball on purpose before, what hope have you got?

Your chances are far better if you can say these magic words: "I've hit this shot before." That means working on your techniques for tough shots — not just a couple of times but until they feel familiar. That way, you're not guessing and hoping when it counts. You're trying to repeat past successes.

Positivity

Before every swing, picture a great result. This practice is more than optimism; it's science! Sports psychologists teach visualization for one simple reason: It works. Just as negative thoughts can derail your swing, positive thoughts — and images — can and do help you hit the ball better. So make picturing a great shot part of your pre-swing routine.

Giving Yourself the Best Shot: Preparing for Each Round

You know the basics of the game. You've got the right equipment, you know your way around different sorts of courses, and you've developed a swing that suits your body and soul. You're ready to get out there and put all your skills to the test.

After you prepare a few handy excuses for stuff that may go wrong for you on the course, you're ready to warm up your body. Warm-ups are important. A few simple exercises not only loosen your muscles and help your swing but also help you psychologically. I like to step onto the first tee knowing that I'm as ready as I can be.

Loosening up

Johnny Bench, the great Cincinnati Reds catcher, showed me the following stretches. He used them when he played baseball, and he's in the Hall of Fame — so who am I to argue?

Holding a club by the head, place the grip end in your armpit so that the shaft runs the length of your arm (use a club that's the same length as your arm for this one, as shown in Figure 9-1). This action stretches your arm and shoulders. Now bend forward until your arm is horizontal. The forward movement stretches your lower back, one of the most important areas in your body when it comes to playing golf. If your back is stiff, you have a hard time making a full turn on the backswing. Hold this position for a few seconds and then switch arms; repeat this stretch until you feel loose enough to swing.

Holding the club like this, bend forward.

Then switch arms and do it again.

Figure 9-1: Stretch before you swing.

Another method of loosening up is more traditional. Instead of practicing your swing with one club in your hands, double the load by swinging two clubs. Go slowly, trying to make as full a back-and-through swing as you can. The extra weight soon stretches away any tightness.

This next exercise is one that many players use on the first tee. Place a club across your back and hold it steady with your hands or elbows. Then turn back and through as if making a golf swing, as shown in Figure 9-2. Again, this action really stretches your back muscles.

Stand as if at address, a club behind your back. Then turn back...

and through.

Figure 9-2: Watch your back!

Warming up your swing

I'm one of those players who likes to schedule about an hour for pre-round practice. But half that time is probably enough for anyone playing a casual game.

You really need to hit only enough balls to build a feel and a rhythm for the upcoming round. Don't make any last-minute changes to your swing.

Start your warm-up by hitting a few short wedge shots. Don't go straight to your driver and start blasting away. That's asking for trouble. You can easily pull a muscle if you swing too hard too soon. Plus, you probably aren't going to immediately hit long, straight drives if you don't warm up first. More likely, you'll hit short, crooked shots. And those are hazardous to a golfer's mental health.

The following steps lead you through a good swing warm-up. *Remember:* You're just warming up. Focus on rhythm and timing — not on the ball.

1. **Start with the wedge.**

   Focus on making solid contact. Nothing else. Try to turn your shoulders a little more with each shot. Hit about 20 balls without worrying about where they're going. Just swing smoothly.

2. **Move to your midirons.**

   I like to hit my 6-iron at this point. I'm just about warmed up, and the 6-iron has just enough loft that I don't have to work too hard to get the ball flying forward. Again, hit about 20 balls.

3. **Hit the driver.**

   Now you're warmed up enough for the big stick. I recommend that you hit no more than a dozen drivers. Getting carried away with this club is easy, and when you go overboard, your swing can get a little quick.

4. **Before you leave the range, hit a few more balls with your wedge.**

   You're not looking for distance with this club, only smoothness.

5. **Finally, spend about ten minutes on the practice putting green.**

   You need to get a feel for the pace of the greens. Start with short uphill putts of two to three feet. Get your confidence and then proceed to longer putts of 20 to 30 feet. After that, practice putting to opposite fringes to get the feeling of speed. Focus on pace rather than direction. You're ready now — head for the first tee!

Correcting Common Problem Shots

Most bad shots result from a handful of common errors. Fortunately, they're fixable. Here's how to beat back the gremlins that can creep into your game.

Slicing

Most golfers *slice* the ball, which means that it starts moving toward the left of the target and finishes to the right. Slices are weak shots that don't go very far. In general, slicers use too much body action, especially upper body, and not enough hand action in their swings.

If you're a slicer, you need to get your hands working in the swing. Here's how:

1. **Address a ball as you normally do.**

   Address is the position of your body just before you begin to swing.

2. **Turn your whole body until your butt is toward the target and your feet are perpendicular to the target line.**

3. **Twist your upper body to the left so that you can again place the clubhead behind the ball.**

   Don't move your feet. From this position, you have in effect made turning your body to your left on the through-swing impossible (see Figure 9-3).

If you slice, try this drill: Stand with your back to the target. Then turn your whole body until your butt is to the target and twist your upper body to address the ball.

1

Swing back...

2

and then swing your hands and arms through...

3

to finish. The ball should fly from right to left.

4

Figure 9-3: Extra hand action cures the slice.

Try it. Should I call a chiropractor yet? The only way you can swing the club through the ball is by using your hands and arms.

4. **Hit a few balls.**

   Focus on letting the toe of the clubhead pass your heel through impact. Quite a change in your ball flight, eh? Because your hands and arms are doing so much of the rotating work in your new swing, the clubhead is doing the same. The clubhead is now closing as it swings through the impact area. The spin imparted on the ball now causes a slight right-to-left flight — something I bet you thought you'd never see.

After you've hit about 20 shots using this drill, switch to your normal stance and try to reproduce the feel you had standing in that strange but correct way. You'll soon be hitting hard, raking *draws* (slight hooks) far up the fairway.

Hooking

Golfers prone to *hooks* (shots that start right and finish left) have the opposite problem of slicers — too much hand action and not enough body. Here's a variation on the earlier drill if you tend to hook the ball:

1. **Adopt your regular stance.**

2. **Turn your whole body until you're looking directly at the target.**

3. **Twist your upper body to the right — don't move your feet — until you can set the clubhead behind the ball (see Figure 9-4).**

4. **Hit some shots.**

   Solid contact is easiest to achieve when you turn your body hard to the left, which prevents your hands from becoming overactive. Your ball flight will soon be a gentle *fade* (slight slice).

If you hit hooks, try this drill: Stand with both feet facing the target. Then turn your upper body until you are facing the target.

Swing back...

and then turn your body in concert with the club...

to finish. The ball should fly from left to right.

Figure 9-4: Extra body action straightens your hook.

After about 20 shots, hit some balls from your normal stance, practicing the technique in the exercise. Reproduce the feel of this drill, and you're that much closer to a successful swing.

Popping up your tee shots

One of the most common sights I see on the first tee of an amateur game is the *skied* tee shot — the ball goes higher than it goes forward. The golfer usually hits the ball on the top part of the driver, causing an ugly mark to appear, which is one reason a tour player never lets an amateur use his driver.

If you're hitting the ball on the top side of your driver, you're swinging the club on too much of a downward arc. What's that mean, you ask? It means that your head is too far in front of the ball (toward the target side of the ball) and your left shoulder is too low at impact.

Here's what to do:

1. **Go find an upslope.**

2. **Stand so that your left foot (if you're right-handed) is higher than your right.**

3. **Tee the ball up and hit drivers or 3-woods until you get the feeling of staying back and under the shot.**

   The uphill lie promotes this feeling.

Here's a secret: People who hit down on their drivers want to kill the stupid ball in front of their buddies. These golfers have a tremendous shift of weight to the left side on the downswing. If you hit balls from an upslope, you can't get your weight to the left side as quickly. Consequently, you keep your head behind the ball, and your left shoulder goes up at impact. Practice on an upslope until you get a feel and then proceed to level ground. You'll turn your pop-ups into line drives.

Suffering from a power outage

Every golfer in the world wants more distance. For that, you need more power. Here's how to make it happen:

✓ **Turn your shoulders on the backswing.** The more you turn your shoulders on the backswing, the better chance you have to hit the ball longer. So really stretch that torso on the backswing — try to put your left shoulder over your right foot at the top of your swing. Thinking that you're turning your back to the target may help.

If you're having difficulty moving your shoulders enough on the backswing, try turning your left knee clockwise until it's pointing behind the ball during your backswing. This setup frees your hips, and subsequently your shoulders, to turn. A big turn starts from the ground up.

✓ **Get the tension out of your grip.** Hold the club loosely; you should grip it with the pressure of holding a spotted owl's egg. If you have too much tension in your hands, your forearms and chest tighten up, and you lose that valuable flexibility that helps with the speed of your arms and hands.

Turning your hips to the left on the downswing and extending your right arm on the throughswing are trademarks of the longer hitters. Here's a drill to help you accomplish this feat of daring:

1. **Tee up your driver in the normal position.**

2. **Place the ball off your left heel and/or opposite your left armpit.**

3. **Now reach down, not moving your stance, and move the ball toward the target the length of the grip.**

4. **Tee up the ball there; it should be about a foot closer to the hole.**

5. **Address the ball where the normal position was and swing at the ball that's now teed up.**

    To hit that ball, you have to move your hips to the left so your arms can reach the ball, and this leads you to extend your right arm.

Practice this drill 20 times. Then put the ball back in the normal position. You should feel faster with the hips and feel a tremendous extension of your right arm.

Shanking

Shanks can strike when you least expect, sending the ball squirting sideways while you shake your fist at the golf gods.

A *shank* (also called a *pitchout,* a *Chinese hook, El Hosel,* a *scud,* or a *snake killer*) occurs when the ball strikes the hosel of the club and goes 90 degrees to the right of your intended target. (The *hosel* is the neck of the club, where the shaft attaches to the clubhead.) Shanks attack the very soul of a golfer. They come unannounced and invade the decorum of a well-played round. They leave with equal haste and lurk in the mind of the golfer, dwelling until the brain reaches critical mass. Then you have meltdown. To a golfer, no other word strikes terror and dread like *shank.*

But don't despair! You can cure the shank!

Shankers almost always set up too close to the ball, with their weight back on their heels. As they shift forward during the swing, their weight comes off their heels, moving the club even closer to the ball, so that the hosel hits the ball.

When you shank, the *heel* of your club (the closest
part of the clubhead to you) continues toward the
target and ends up right of the target. To eliminate
shanks, you need the toe of the club to go toward the
target and end up left of the target.

 Here's an easy exercise (shown in Figure 9-5)
that helps cure the shanks:

1. **Get a two-by-four and align it along your target
   line.**

   You can also use a cardboard box.

2. **Put the ball two inches from the near edge of
   the board and try to hit the ball.**

   If you shank the shot, your club wants to hit the
   board. If you swing properly, the club comes
   from the inside and hits the ball. Then the toe
   of the club goes left of the target, the ball goes
   straight, and your woes are over (shanking ones
   anyway).

Missing too many short putts

Some people argue that putting is more mental than
physical. But before you resort to séances with your
local psychic, check your alignment. You can often
trace missed putts to poor aim.

 You can work on alignment in many ways, but
my colleague Peter Kostis invented a device
called The Putting Professor to help straighten
out troubled putters. It's similar to an old, tried-
and-true putting aid, the string between two
rods, which helped golfers keep the putter going
straight back and straight through impact
toward the hole. Straight as a string, get it?

Release the toe and don't hit the board.

Figure 9-5: Just say, "No shanks!"

But Peter had a better idea. The Putting Professor features a plexiglass panel and a metal bar that attaches to your putter (see Figure 9-6). Keep the bar in contact with the plexiglass as you practice, and you groove a smooth stroke that keeps the face of your putter square to the target. This stroke is particularly important on those knee-knocking short putts.

Of course, you can't use such a device during a round of golf. But after you develop the right stroke on the practice green, you can repeat it on the course — and watch those putts roll straight and true.

Figure 9-6: The Putting Professor keeps a putter's face square to the target.

An important lesson you can learn with devices like The Putting Professor is the crucial relationship between the putter's face and the target line. Putting takes an imagination: If you can picture the line and keep the face of your putter square to it, stroking the ball along that line to the hole is easy.

Weathering the Elements

When conditions on the golf course are rough because of wind or rain, scores go up. Adjust your goals. Don't panic if you start off badly or have a couple of poor holes. Be patient and realize that sometimes conditions make golf even harder. And remember that bad weather is equally tough on all the other players.

A calm head and good management skills are just as important as hitting the ball solidly when you're trying to get through tough days in the wind and rain.

Handling high winds

I remember playing the TPC Championship at Sawgrass in the late 1980s on one of the windiest days we'd ever seen. J. C. Snead hit a beautiful downwind approach to an elevated green. Somehow the ball stopped on the green with the wind blowing upwards of 50 miles per hour. J. C. was walking toward the green when his Panama hat blew off. He chased it, only to watch the hat blow onto the green and hit his golf ball! That's a two-shot penalty, and rotten luck.

If the wind is blowing hard, try these tips:

✓ **Widen your stance to lower your center of gravity.** This change automatically makes your swing shorter (for control) because turning your body is more difficult when your feet are set wider apart. (Figure 9-7 illustrates this stance.)

✓ **Swing easier.** I always take a less-lofted club than normal and swing easier. This way, I have a better chance of hitting the ball squarely. By hitting the ball squarely, I minimize the wind's effects.

✓ **Use the wind — don't fight it.** Let the ball go where the wind wants it to go. If the wind is blowing left-to-right at 30 miles per hour, aim left and let the wind bring your ball back. Don't aim right and try to hook it back into the wind. Leave that to the airline pilots and the guys on the PGA Tour!

✓ **Choke down on the club.** You don't have to keep your left hand (for right-handed golfers) all the way at the top of the grip. Move it down an inch. This grip gives you more control. Keeping my left hand about one inch from the top of the grip gives me more control over the club and the direction of the shot it hits. But more control comes with a cost: The ball doesn't go as far as it would if I used the full length of the shaft.

✔ **Allow for more run downwind and shorter flight against the wind.** You have to experience this part of the game to understand it. The more you play in windy conditions, the more comfortable you become.

A wide stance helps you keep your balance in a breeze.

Figure 9-7: Windy means wider.

Swingin' in the rain

The best advice I can give you for playing in the rain is to make like a Boy Scout and *be prepared*. For starters, pack the right all-weather gear including an umbrella, rain gear (that means jackets, pants, and headwear designed to be worn in the rain), dry gloves, towels, dry grips, waterproof shoes, and an extra pair of dry socks in case the advertiser lied about those "waterproof" shoes.

A golf course changes significantly in the rain. You need to adjust your game accordingly:

✔ On a rainy day, the greens are slow. Hit your putts harder and remember that the ball doesn't curve as much. You can also be more aggressive on approach shots to the greens.

✔ If you hit a ball into a bunker, remember that wet sand is firmer than dry sand. You don't have to swing as hard to get the ball out.

✔ A wet golf course plays longer because it's soft — a 400-yard hole seems more like 450. The good news here is that the fairways and greens become, in effect, wider and bigger, because your shots don't bounce into trouble as much as they would on a dry day. That means you can afford to take more club — and more chances.

✔ Try not to let the conditions affect your normal routines. The best rain players always take their time and stay patient.

✔ Playing in the rain is one thing; playing in lightning is another altogether. Here's my tip on playing in lightning: *Don't.* When lightning strikes, your metallic golf club (along with the fact that you tend to be the highest point on the golf course, unless a tree is nearby) can make you a target. So when you see lightning, don't take chances — take cover.

Chapter 10

Golf's Ten Commandments

* *

In This Chapter
▶ Taking steps to play your best
▶ Observing golf etiquette

* *

*H*aving been around golf for a while, I've racked my feeble brain and jotted down ten tips to keep you from suffering the same cataclysms I see on golf courses all over the world. Knowing not to repeat these errors can help you live a long and peaceful life on the links.

Take Some Golf Lessons

If you really want to have fun playing this game, start off with a few lessons to get you on the right track. It's amazing what you can do with a clear concept of how to make a golf swing. And, of course, read this book in its entirety.

Use a Club That Can Get You to the Hole

I'm constantly playing with amateurs who come up short with their approach shots to the green. For whatever reason, they always choose a club that can get the shot only to the front of the green — even if they hit the most solid shot of their lives. You can play smarter than they do: Take a club that you can swing at 80 percent and still get to the hole. Conserve your energy; you have a long life ahead of you!

If You Can Putt the Ball, Do It

Don't always use a *lofted* club (a wedge or other iron designed to hit the ball high) around the greens. Instead, whenever you can, use a less-lofted club that gets the ball rolling as soon as possible.

Keep Your Head Fairly Steady

Your head should move a little during the swing, especially with the longer clubs. But try not to move it too much. Moving your head too much leads to all sorts of serious swing flaws. Have someone watch or film you to see how much you move your head.

Be Kind to the Course

In fairways, replace your divot or fill it in with *divot mix,* the mixture of sand and grass seed you find in plastic jugs attached to golf carts. On the green, use a divot-repair tool to fix the mark your ball made when it landed. (Left untended, a ball mark can take two or three weeks to heal, while one that's fixed can be good as new in three or four days.) And for good measure, fix one other ball mark, too. You'll be a hero to other golfers and to the greenskeeper!

Bet Only What You Can Afford to Lose

You can lose friends by betting for more money than you have. Never bet what you can't afford to lose. My strategy was always to bet everything in my pocket except for $10 — enough to pay for the gas I'd need to get home.

Keep the Ball Low in the Wind

When the wind starts to kick up, you need to adapt. Play the ball back in your stance, put your hands ahead of the ball, and keep them ahead of the ball at impact. Keep the ball as low as you can, and you manage your game much more efficiently. You probably won't lose as many golf balls, either.

Don't Give Lessons to Your Spouse

Giving golf lessons to your spouse should be a federal offense. Don't try it! Doing so can only lead to disaster. Invest some money in lessons from a pro instead. Get your spouse good instruction and reap the benefit: peace of mind.

Always Tee It Up at a Tee Box

Whenever it's legal (in the teeing area), tee the ball up. This game is more fun when the ball is in the air. As Jack Nicklaus once said, "Through years of experience I have learned that air offers less resistance than dirt."

Keep Your Wits

If all else fails, if you lose your last golf ball, you can keep your sense of humor and survive. ***Remember:*** This game is hard enough without blaming yourself for everything. Or for anything! I like to blame my bad shots on magnetic fields from alien spacecraft. Which leads me to one of golf's eternal questions: What's *your* excuse?

Math & Science

Algebra I For Dummies,
2nd Edition
978-0-470-55964-2

Biology For Dummies,
2nd Edition
978-0-470-59875-7

Chemistry For Dummies,
2nd Edition
978-1-1180-0730-3

Geometry For Dummies,
2nd Edition
978-0-470-08946-0

Pre-Algebra Essentials
For Dummies
978-0-470-61838-7

Microsoft Office

Excel 2010 For Dummies
978-0-470-48953-6

Office 2010 All-in-One
For Dummies
978-0-470-49748-7

Office 2011 for Mac
For Dummies
978-0-470-87869-9

Word 2010
For Dummies
978-0-470-48772-3

Music

Guitar For Dummies,
2nd Edition
978-0-7645-9904-0

Clarinet For Dummies
978-0-470-58477-4

iPod & iTunes
For Dummies, 9th Edition
978-1-118-13060-5

Pets

Cats For Dummies,
2nd Edition
978-0-7645-5275-5

Dogs All-in-One
For Dummies
978-0470-52978-2

Saltwater Aquariums
For Dummies,
2nd Edition
978-0-470-06805-2

Religion & Inspiration

The Bible For Dummies
978-0-7645-5296-0

Catholicism
For Dummies,
2nd Edition
978-1-118-07778-8

Spirituality For Dummies,
2nd Edition
978-0-470-19142-2

Self-Help & Relationships

Happiness For Dummies
978-0-470-28171-0

Overcoming Anxiety
For Dummies,
2nd Edition
978-0-470-57441-6

Seniors

Crosswords For Seniors
For Dummies
978-0-470-49157-7

iPad For Seniors
For Dummies, 2nd Edition
978-1-118-03827-7

Laptops & Tablets
For Seniors
For Dummies,
2nd Edition
978-1-118-09596-6

Smartphones & Tablets

BlackBerry
For Dummies, 5th Edition
978-1-118-10035-6

Droid X2 For Dummies
978-1-118-14864-8

HTC ThunderBolt
For Dummies
978-1-118-07601-9

MOTOROLA XOOM
For Dummies
978-1-118-08835-7

Sports

Basketball For Dummies,
3rd Edition
978-1-118-07374-2

Football For Dummies,
4th Edition
978-1-118-01261-1

Golf For Dummies,
4th Edition
978-0-470-88279-5

Test Prep

ACT For Dummies,
5th Edition
978-1-118-01259-8

ASVAB For Dummies,
3rd Edition
978-0-470-63760-9

The GRE Test
For Dummies, 7th Edition
978-0-470-00919-2

Police Officer Exam
For Dummies
978-0-470-88724-0

Series 7 Exam
For Dummies
978-0-470-09932-2

Web Development

HTML, CSS, & XHTML
For Dummies, 7th Edition
978-0-470-91659-9

Drupal For Dummies,
2nd Edition
978-1-118-08348-2

Windows 7

Windows 7
For Dummies
978-0-470-49743-2

Windows 7
For Dummies,
Book + DVD Bundle
978-0-470-52398-8

Windows 7 All-in-One
For Dummies
978-0-470-48763-1

Wherever you are in life, Dummies makes it easier.

From fashion to Facebook®, wine to Windows®, and everything in between, Dummies makes it easier.

 Visit us at Dummies.com and connect with us online at www.facebook.com/fordummies or @fordummies